The

Snowboarder's

Total Guide

to Life

BILL KERIG

VILLARD ❖ NEW YORK

The Snowboarder's Total Guide to Life

VILLARD BOOKS is a registered trademark of Random House, Inc.

Library of Congress Cataloging-in-Publication Data

Kerig, Bill.
The snowboarder's total guide to life / Bill Kerig.
p.   cm.
ISBN 0-375-75048-7 (alk. paper)
1. Snowboarding—Humor. I. Title.
PN6231.S627K47   1998
818'.5407—dc21   97-28503

Original illustrations by Michael Kupperman
Photographs on pp. 138 and 140 by Dann Coffey
All other photographs courtesy AP/World Wide Photos

Random House website address: www.randomhouse.com
Printed in the United States of America on acid-free paper
24689753
First Edition

ACKNOWLEDGMENTS

To Jennifer Webb, Melissa Milsten, Laurence Kerig, Daniel Rembert, and ICM's Jack Horner: Thanks for spending serious time so that I could have such silly fun writing this.

CONTENTS

Acknowledgments   v
Introduction   xi

Book I: Who and What Is a Snowboarder?
  1. The Species: North American Snowboarder
     (*Singleplankus ripthehillicus*)   4
  2. Board Betty and Bro   10
  3. Subspecies: Jibber (*Singleplankus r.
     spinnicus*)   21
  4. Subspecies: Carver (*Singleplankus r. arcus*)   25
  5. Subspecies: Instructor (*Singleplankus r.
     teachthechumpsicus*)   31
  6. Subspecies: Shop Rat (*Singleplankus r.
     shopraticus*)   37

Contents

7. Subspecies: Tourist (*Singleplankus r. rentalnightmaris*)   42
8. Subspecies: Pro Bro (*Singleplankus r. paidforplayicus*)   46

Book II: Behavior of the Snowboarder
9. Grooming Habits of the Snowboarder   55
10. Feeding Habits of the Snowboarder   59
11. Courtship and Mating Rituals of the Snowboarder   63
12. Plumage of the Snowboarder   74
13. Ornamentation of the Snowboarder   84
14. Symbols of the Snowboard Culture   89
15. Popular Art of the Snowboard Culture   92

Book III: Where Did the Snowboarder Come From, and Where Is He/She Now?
16. The Snowboard Creation Myth   99
17. Evolution and the Snowboarder   107
18. The Snowboarder's Habitat   111
19. Migratory Patterns   116
20. Favored Transportation of the Snowboarder   121

Book IV: How to Become a Snowboarder
21. Adopting the Right Attitude   127
22. How to Talk the Talk   131

23. How to Walk the Walk 134
24. How to Carry a Snowboard 137
25. The Cool Daddy Handshake 139
26. How to Choose Sunglasses 142
27. How to Move to the Mountains 145

Book V: Tips for the Non-Snowboarder
28. How to Have a Relationship with a
   Snowboarder 155
29. How to Rent a House to a Snowboarder . . . 162
30. How to Raise a Snowboarder (Without
   It Ending Up in Jail) 166
31. How to Employ a Snowboarder 169

The Snowboarder's Ten Commandments 171
Glossary 173
North American Snowboard Spotter Checklist . 183
An Exhaustive List of Snowboarder
   Contributions to Society 185

High in the snow-covered mountains of North America a new and strange species of *Homo sapiens* is mutating. Characterized by wide, boardlike appendages that attach to its feet, this new species has created a language, a community, a world around the act of riding a buttered stick down a slippery slope.

The scientific name for this species is *Single-plankus ripthehillicus*. That's Snowboarder to you and me. And I must admit, I'm one of them.

"My name is Bill and I'm a Snowboarder" is how the 12-Step program would begin. That is, if there were a 12-Step program for un-becoming a Snowboarder. There isn't.

Primarily because once a human has become a Snowboarder, no amount of "One day at a time" or "Easy does it" could un-Snowboard him/her. I know, I've tried.

After years in baggy snowboard pants, I attempted to shimmy into trousers that fit like John Travolta's in *Saturday Night Fever.* I tried to un-pierce the parts of me that bear holes. I sold my Sims, fled the mountains, got a "real job."

Then it snowed.

The first flake for a Snowboarder is like a taste of Guinness to an Irish drunk. It hits your tongue and it's all over. Told my wife I was going for a quart of milk and didn't stop till I got to Mammoth.

Before you could say Betty Ford I was blissfully carving, flipping to fakie, boning it out.

My non-Snowboarder friends took me off their E-mail lists, ripped my card from their Rolodexes. The six-figure salary in the city was history (okay, I never had one, but if I had . . .).

Then it came to me: Instead of kicking the habit, I'd embrace the addiction. I'd preach it, spread the 'board word wherever man had ears to listen.

It's now my belief that every man, woman, and child has the inalienable right to wear baggies.

Every one of God's children deserves to be baptized with BIG air.

Two boards in every garage. Airwalks in every backseat. A tattoo on every ankle.

You don't have to be young, hip, or hairy. We can all be Snowboarders.

Don't get me wrong, however. Living a total Snowboarder's life isn't easy. You don't just throw on a pair of baggies and start saying "brah" a lot. Whooooa no. There's a whole lot more to it than that.

Being a Snowboarder is a total thang. It's not a sport, it's a cult. It's not an adventure, it's an acid trip.

Wanna ride along? Better know the secret knock, talk the talk, perform the Cool Daddy Handshake.

That's where I come in.

I'll decipher the Snowboarder's argot, take you to visit a typical lair, explain migratory patterns and grooming habits, and investigate the wild courtship and mating rituals of the Snowboarder. I'll lay bare the secret myths of the Snowboarder, explore the symbolism of the stick, ferret out the facts (but by no means be limited by them) of the Snowboarder's formula. Most important, I'll give you the skinny on how to be phat.

BOOK I

Who and What Is a Snowboarder?

The Species:
North American
Snowboarder
(Singleplankus ripthehillicus)

There are eight subspecies in the mammalian category *Singleplankus ripthehillicus*. A species of *Homo sapiens*** (though some would argue this point), all breed or have bred in the snowy regions of North America, where the necessity of bodily contact for warmth has led to a huge population explosion of this strange strain.

The *Singleplankus ripthehillicus* is characterized by a flat, boardlike growth formed between its two feet that extends sometimes as much as 50

---

* A fancy Latin name for you and me. No cause for homo phobic alarm.

centimeters in front and behind its metatarsal digits. Although this growth may have evolved to facilitate movement on snow, it's just as likely the North American Snowboarder has *chosen* to attach this planklike extension to its feet for purposes of rebellion, inclusion, or a primitive desire to hunch over and hop like an ape across flat sections of snow.

The *Singleplankus ripthehillicus* can actually detach the boardlike appendage at will. Once it is removed, the Snowboarder can perambulate much like other species of *Homo sapiens*. Yet removing the board is a huge demerit on the social scoreboard of the *Singleplankus ripthehillicus*. Boardotomies* are performed only in the most dire of circumstances and usually under heavy sedation.

In addition to its boardlike appendage, the North American Snowboarder has many other telling traits. For one, its facial coloring is mottled. The chin, cheeks, and forehead are brown

---

* Similar to lobotomies. Instead of removing the brain, however, the board is removed. For a Snowboarder, this is much more disastrous and, unlike a lobotomy, it makes Snowboarder socializing nearly impossible.

or deep red, while a figure-eight pattern on the skin adjacent to the eyes is pale and often white. The ears of the Snowboarder are also a deep brown or red in color, battered and scabbed—a lot like day-old buffalo carpaccio.*

Hands are another telling trait. Digits will appear crooked (as a result of frequent breakage and splinting by taping them to beer bottles). Oversized thumbs (from jamming their hands into the snow in efforts to avert calamitous impact with terra firma) are a sign that a *Homo sapiens* is a Snowboarder.

There are many other traits of the North American Snowboarder (discussed more thoroughly in the following pages as they relate to each subspecies), but none is more telling than the slippery, and oft difficult to identify demeanor of the Snowboarder. This is what truly makes a Snowboarder a Snowboarder.

The Snowboarder just looks at life differently from other *Homo sapiens*. The following chart shows the difference in the hierarchy of needs:

* The name for thin strips of tough, dried-out buffalo meat that chichi restaurants charge $12 for.

Homo sapiens	Singleplankus ripthehillicus
1. Food	1. Snow
2. Shelter	2. Hill
3. Warmth	3. Snowboard
4. Love	4. Food
5. Automobile	5. Sex

These differences make the Snowboarder behave very differently from most other humans. The average *Homo sapiens* will kill, fight, and plunder to provide food and shelter for its clan; the North American Snowboarder will take a job at a resort Taco Bell (nights only) to provide for all its needs.

The Beatles may have been right in their assessment that "money can't buy me love,"* but the *Singleplankus ripthehillicus* is more apt to say, "Love can't buy me a sweet ride."

Whereas diplomas, MBAs, and mortgages are necessary totems for many *Homo sapiens,* the

---

* From a pathetically naive song of the 1960s. In the 1990s Hugh Grant has shown that money can buy not only love but also a tremendous amount of press and the resurrection of a flailing career.

season pass is the Snowboarder's badge of honor. Boffo bank accounts, platinum credit cards, and thick wads of cash are tokens of success for many North American humans. The *Singleplankus ripthehillicus* tallies achievement by the number of sponsorship stickers that are affixed to its boardlike appendage.

The North American Snowboarder may be difficult for the novice to identify when seen outside its habitat, but with careful attention to detail, the Snowboard spotter can pick out a Snowboarder, even in unlikely environs (libraries, museums, or classrooms).

Yes, the *Singleplankus ripthehillicus* is a different breed, one of the most recently evolved species in the family of man. But let us not dismiss the North American Snowboarder with sweeping generalizations. Let us take a look at the specifics of the subspecies of the *Single-plankus ripthehillicus.*

Then we'll dismiss them.

CHAPTER 2

Board Betty
and Bro

North American Snowboarders fall into two cat-
egories: the Board Betty (the female of the
species) and the Board Bro (the male).

Although many traits differ from one subspecies (Carver, Jibber, Instructor, et cetera) to
the next, each gender shares certain prerequisite
characteristics. As Bettys and Bros look pretty
much the same when riding the hill, one must
view the *Singleplankus ripthehillicus* in settings
where it feels comfortable enough to remove its
tentlike outer garments. These settings include
coffeehouses, bars, and jail.

THE BOARD BETTY

The Board Betty could be a Salvation Army poster girl. Not because she's so in need of food or donations (most Board Bettys have pleasingly voluptuous frames) but because her entire wardrobe looks as if it's been plucked from a Salvation Army truck.

The Board Betty gets her fashion inspiration from Nick at Nite reruns of *The Partridge Family,* *The Brady Bunch,* and *Welcome Back, Kotter.* For this reason the hair of the Board Betty will always be bobbed and curled into a mock-1970s flip.

She will always wear a tight-fitting sweater or T-shirt with a horizontal stripe across her breasts. The sweater can be either a mothball-smelling ski

sweater circa Richard Nixon or a high-priced patchouli-smelling clone from a too-hip boutique. The two are virtually indistinguishable.

The sweater or T-shirt will ride up on her stomach to reveal a pierced navel. This will also reveal the top of her men's boxer shorts.

Several inches below the top of her boxer shorts, her jeans will droop as if clinging to her hips by the tiniest of threads. Her jeans may either balloon out like her snowboard pants or hug her thighs before descending into bell-bottoms. Either way they will be faded and aerated with gaping holes. They may be patched with multi-colored bandanna fabric.

Beneath the flapping bell-bottoms of the Board Betty's trousers, and above her clogs or platform shoes (with knobby black soles that could withstand an Everest hike), there will be a small ankle tattoo. This may be a yin-yang symbol, a moon, or a Burton logo. An anklet made from a severed snowboard leash is optional.

Pierced tongues, necklaces made of metal beads (like oversized key rings), or nose rings are also optional, but there is one aspect of the Board Betty's character that is completely mandatory.

Contrary to popular belief, it is not the presence of copious hair under her armpits.

The characteristic a Board Betty *must* possess is slouching posture. A Board Betty must look like the Wicked Witch of the West in *The Wizard of Oz* just after Dorothy's thrown the bucket of water on her. A successful Board Betty will always look as if she were just about to melt down into a puddle of plasma, without ever quite dissolving.

Many anthropologists believe that the evolution of the *Singleplankus ripthehillicus* has left the Board Betty with a jellied spine, but this is not the case. It's actually her knees that have jellied. From spending so much time standing on a slip-

pery slat, the Board Betty's knees are in permanent flex. They cannot straighten. This gives the Board Betty not only fantastic balance on her snowboard but also an uncanny ability to remain standing during calamitous Los Angeles earthquakes and New York City subway rides.

THE BOARD BRO

The Board Bro is characterized by a shiny, opaque film that covers his eyes. This film is ringed with a hard, dark-colored frame. Most people assume this optical attachment is merely a pair of sunglasses. It may have been at some time, but it has now become *part* of the Board Bro. He cannot remove it.

Growing out and around this permanently affixed facial accessory are sprouts of hair shaved into strange and interesting patterns. Some hair will grow from his chin, more down his jawline. While most think these sideburns and goatee are fashion statements, they are actually cosmetic cover-ups.

For the Board Bro's chin when seen hairless is revealed to be scarred from plowing icy snow in

the snowboard initiation ritual known as the face plant.* His jaw will also be pockmarked from another hazing ritual known as "the eggbeater."† Recurring waking nightmares of these two rituals explain the lip-twisting grimace that the Board Bro exhibits.

The Board Bro wears a necklace. This may be leather, the other half of his Board Betty's shorn snowboard leash, or a dead snake.

The Board Bro will also wear boxer shorts sticking out from his jeans (unless he is engaged to the Board Betty, which means she now possesses all his boxers and he'll be "going commando").‡

Decidedly low-tech sneakers are part of the Board Bro's uniform. These may be authentic Keds, Converse All Stars, or the more prevalent Simples.§

The Board Bro also dangles accessories from his frame. Wallet chains are popular, although

---

* The act of driving one's head into the snow. The only things that grow from this planting are welts.
† A fall in which the Snowboarder's head slams repeatedly against the ground, thereby scrambling his eggs.
‡ Bareback. Without underwear.
§ A brand of sneaker that's manufactured by a monstrous shoe company named Dexter that advertises itself as a "nice little shoe company," thereby underscoring the Board Bro's marketing gullibility.

chaining a wallet that contains only $3 and a condom may be seen as a bit of overkill.* Some might also view nose rings and tongue studs as overkill, but not the Board Bro.

The more things he can hang off himself (chains, bracelets, pine-tree-shaped car deodorizers), the more attractive the Board Bro makes himself to the Board Betty. For this reason many a Board Betty has become confused and taken to dating her Christmas tree.

BETTY AND BRO ACCESSORIES
• A backpack. Should contain a roll of toilet paper stolen from the midmountain restaurant, a pack of cigarettes (even if he/she doesn't smoke), a lighter, condoms (women's pack only), and a copy of this book.
• A ball cap with what looks like a John Deere (tractor) logo but really is a snowboard company's emblem.
• A key chain with something kitschy attached (like a mini R2-D2).†

---

* A lot like the chains affixed to pens at the bank.
† The little robot in *Star Wars* that cruised around with a Snowboarder stance and spoke a language as indecipherable as the Snowboarder's.

• The daily paper with listings of happy hours and all-you-can-eat buffets circled in crayon.

CHAPTER 3

Subspecies: Jibber

(Singleplankus r. spinnicus)

The *Singleplankus r. spinnicus* is the court jester of the North American Snowboarder species. As such it is the most fun to view in its native habitat. Defined by loose-fitting skins and a duck-footed stance,* the *Singleplankus r. spinnicus* performs the most elaborately of any subspecies of North American Snowboarder.

While a Jibber doesn't have to be chronologically young, its mind-set seems to be permanently stuck at age thirteen. Often the baby or a change-

---

* Toes facing out, away from each other. Because of the way this stance tends to stick the Jibber's hindquarters out, into the wind, it's also known as "Stinky."

of-life child, the *Singleplankus r. spinnicus* was neglected by its early snowboarding family.*

Thus the *Singleplankus r. spinnicus* is always looking for someone to impress. For this reason it seeks out the most populated haunts of the North American Snowboarder: the halfpipe and park.

Once there, the *Singleplankus r. spinnicus* isn't happy just performing for other Jibbers and Snowboard spotters that happen to be looking its way. It must be the center of attention. To accomplish this, it periodically slaps its board against hard objects (trees, rails, ski instructors' heads) to make a loud noise. The Jibber will then switch from riding forward to backward to forward, just so it can see that everyone is watching.

Next it leaps into the air and spins around to make sure everyone in a 360-degree radius is aware of its presence. Jib- bers that are particularly needy of attention have been known to spin revolu- tions of 540, 720, and even 1,080 degrees. Once the

* Psychobabble for "the kid was a pathetic weenie."

Singleplankus r. spinnicus has everyone's attention—knows for *sure* that every eye is upon it—it stops dead in its tracks, squats on its haunches, lights a cigarette, and strikes a pose meant to tell everyone it is too cool to crave their attention.

It is most unnerving to see a hundred or so Jibbers in a small area. The cacophony from the boards slapping sounds like mortar fire. The smoke from scores of cigarettes is thicker than mustard gas. The whup-whup-whupping of so many spinning boards sounds like a helicopter strike.

In fact, the scene in the snowboard park so closely resembles the surreal Ngong Bridge scene in the film *Apocalypse Now** that many onlookers (especially skiers) have been heard to proclaim, "The world is coming to an end!"

---

* A nightmarish scene that *Apocalypse*'s director, Francis Ford Coppola, witnessed at the snowboard park at Big Bear and wrote during après-ski.

CHAPTER 4

Subspecies: Carver

(Singleplankus r. arcus)

The storm trooper of the North American Snowboard subspecies, the *Singleplankus r. arcus* is
characterized by rigidity and aggression. Its
boardlike appendage is narrow, stiff, and attached to the *Singleplankus r. arcus* with extremely serious clamps that resemble inhumane
animal leghold traps.

To keep these steely jaws from ripping its feet
apart, the *Singleplankus r. arcus* has evolved
hard, shiny shells (also known as carving boots)
over its metatarsal regions.

Descended from the nonevolved two-footed

skigeekicus (also known as a skier),* the *Single-plankus r. arcus* can be spotted from a distance by its skierlike forward-facing profile. Most often dwelling on wide interstate highway–like swatches of smooth snow, the *Singleplankus r.*

---

* An ancient strain of mountain-based *Homo sapiens* that faces imminent extinction.

arcus is not only the most fleet of the *Singleplankus* subspecies but also the vandal. It has a fervent desire to lacerate all that is smooth, to shred all that is whole.

Psychologists* believe the aggressive behavior of the *Singleplankus r. arcus* is a result of repressed shame and guilt stemming from its genetic heritage (remember, it evolved from the reprehensible two-footed skigeekicus).

As a result, the Carver spends its time diving in high-speed falcon arcs at unsuspecting members of the two-footed skigeekicus family. If the *Singleplankus r. arcus* does not actually strike the two-footed skigeekicus, it lays deep trenches to trip it up. Once the two-footed skigeekicus is down, the *Singleplankus r. arcus* will skin it and actually don its costume.

Cloaked in the skins of the two-footed skigeekicus, the Carver can then prey even more effectively on other two-footed skigeekici. Through long sessions on the alpine therapist's chairlift,

---

* A new strain of *Homo sapiens* that has arisen to fill the time-honored listener role of the bartender or priest. They differ from their predecessors in that they charge more, spill less, don't offer peanuts or holy water, but are still largely in the dark about most things.

the *Singleplankus r. arcus* can be dissuaded from this behavior. Unless, of course, it is a member of a more rare and far more deadly subspecies, known as *Singleplankus r. arcus funnytalkicus*. There is no hope of changing this menacing subspecies.

The *Singleplankus r. arcus funnytalkicus* (or EuroCarver) hails from European nesting grounds, therefore it has not only the guilt and shame of its forebears to drive it to destruction and thievery but also a deep wellspring of nationalistic animosity toward all that is North American. Many naively believe the *funnytalkici*'s grudge against all North American snowbound species is a result of envy over the superiority of North American riders.

Yet it's not that simple.

The pain and anguish the *funnytalkicus* feels is much deeper. It stems from an ancient vendetta that is so serious, so dire, that the *funnytalkicus* will never be able—no matter how many North American two-footed skigeekici it fells—to balance its internal scales of justice. The vendetta to which I refer is, of course, the deep-seated desire to make all North Americans *pay* for *Hogan's Heroes*.

It is for this reason that most *Singleplankus r. arcus funnytalkici* take on either the look of Colonel Klink or the much more sinister profile of Major Hochstetter.

CHAPTER 5

Subspecies: Instructor

(Singleplankus r. teachthechumpsicus)

They say that those who can't do anything teach it. Meant to belittle those who endeavor to instruct the young of the species, this malicious one-liner describes those who are not proficient enough at a particular activity to make an honest-to-goodness living with their skill. Thus they are doomed to the lesser role of teaching it.

Nowhere is this tattered cliché less true than in the case of the Professor of the Plank, the *Singleplankus r. teachthechumpsicus.*

For, as all initiates know, the *Singleplankus r. teachthechumpsicus* has no interest whatsoever in teaching. In the hierarchy of the Snowboarder subspecies, the *Singleplankus r. teachthechump-*

sicus performs a far more important role: gatekeeper. If the world of snowboarding is heaven, the *Singleplankus r. teachthechumpsicus* is Saint Peter.*

Not everyone is going to make it into heaven, and likewise not every yahoo that straps a plank to its lower appendages can become a Snowboarder. The *Singleplankus r. teachthechumpsicus*'s job is to dole out the rites of initiation so that only the few, the proud, the brain-dead get in.

For this role the *Singleplankus r. teachthechumpsicus* dons a ceremonial cloak that bears the emblem and logo of the sector it is meant to protect. This logo is embedded into the breast of the plumage. To the uninitiated this may seem as innocuous as the name of the resort where the *Singleplankus r. teachthechumpsicus* seems to work. But be not fooled, dear reader; nothing could be further from the truth. The *Single-*

---

* A hall monitor at the Pearly Gates of Heaven. No good-guy pass, no heaven for you, my friend.

plankus r. teachthechumpsicus does not work for the resort, it labors for a much nobler cause: the perpetuation of its species.

The family of the North American Snowboarder is evolving too quickly to let Darwinian selection* take place willy-nilly. The *Singleplankus r. teachthechumpsicus* must exact a strenuous and brutal initiation ritual upon all who wish to enter the fold.

This hazing ceremony, benignly entitled Snowboard Lesson No. 1, is a daylong beating through which the *Singleplankus r. teachthechumpsicus* puts all comers. In this ceremony the Instructor takes unsuspecting wanna-bes through a series of drills meant to pummel the weak into retreat, to bow and enfeeble the strong.

The *Singleplankus r. teachthechumpsicus* will chant, "Here's how you make a toe-side turn." Which actually means: "Now I'm going to slam you on your face." After repeated frontal body assaults, the Instructor chants, "Let's try the same thing on your heel side."

---

* The process whereby the weak are killed off and only the strong survive. Of course, at the end of the twentieth century this has been supplanted by economical selection—or survival of the fattest.

This, of course, means, "Now we're going to turn you over, like a tough steak, and tenderize your rump." This beating is administered until the sun dips from the sky.

The *Singleplankus r. teachthechumpsicus* will then force the pupil to buy dinner, beer, and tequila while regaling it with hours of uninterrupted babble consisting mostly of the words "dude," "right on," and "brah" (a typical sentence: "Dude, it was like right on, you know, brah?").

This ritual is performed until either the pupil keels over or the sun comes up.

If the newbie returns to the *Singleplankus r. teachthechumpsicus*'s proving ground for a second day of hazing, the Instructor will begin to consider letting it into the fold. First, however, it must acquaint the newcomer with real pain.

"Now, we'll teach you how to ride the trees. Remember, see spaces, not trees," the Instructor will say. Translation: "Bite bark, board boy."

Then there's the mandatory cliff jump, in which the *Singleplankus r. teachthechumpsicus* directs the new rider to sail out into the air. Seasoned members of the species refer to this as the "Schmuck Tuck 'n' Huck phase."

During the second day, if the larva-stage Snowboarder has not run for its lawyer, the *Singleplankus r. teachthechumpsicus* will begin to force-feed it the secret codes and mores of the North American Snowboarder.

At this stage the plebe is suffering from concussion, sprains, abrasions, possible hairline fractures, and a raging hangover. Thus, its brain is squishy, pickled, and unable to resist.

If, after all of this, the student returns for a third day, the *Singleplankus r. teachthechumpsicus* presents it with a hefty bill, a packet of NōDōz, and a Mountain Dew (for the hangover), and proclaims it a Snowboarder.

If it buys beer on the third day, the *Singleplankus r. teachthechumpsicus* will present it with its own ceremonial cloak, making it a fullblown Instructor.

What's the difference between a never-ever and a snowboard instructor?

Three days.

CHAPTER 6

Subspecies: Shop Rat

(Singleplankus r. shopraticus)

Although ubiquitous, the *Singleplankus r. shopraticus* is the hardest member of the North American Snowboarder family to catalog. The principal reason is this subspecies claims not to exist. In fact it will emphatically state that it is something altogether different from a *Singleplankus r. shopraticus*.

This makes this subspecies especially entertaining to stalk and engage. The Snowboard spotter with a little imagination can find the lair of the *Singleplankus r. shopraticus* simply by looking in the yellow pages under "Snowboard Shops." Yet the *Singleplankus r. shopraticus* can just as easily

be found by looking for small storefronts with hundreds of cigarette butts outside the front door, small mountains of empty beer bottles by the back door, and signs emblazoned with cute double-meaning messages such as ONE-TRACK MIND.

After stepping over the mandatory sleeping dog, present at the entrance to every snowboard shop worth its Sex Wax, the first person you'll encounter won't be the *Singleplankus r. shopraticus*.

This species may wear stylin' retro baggies and an old plaid shirt, and be caked with enough

P-tex to fill the Hood River Gorge, but it is not the *Singleplankus r. shopraticus.*

"Do you work here?" you ask.

"Well kinda, dude, whaddya need?"

At this point you know you've found a completely different subspecies: the *Singleplankus r. wannabeicus shopraticus.*

This group roosts in snowboard shops in hopes of trading gnarly stories and a few cigs for free gear. It is not worth your time. Plow on past this pretender.

Move to the back of the shop. Look for a young Board Bro. He will be stretched out over a workbench. He will sip at a Jack and Coke* in a paper 7-Eleven cup. A cigarette will be burned to the filter yet still dangle from his lip.

"Do you work here?" you ask, setting the *Singleplankus r. shopraticus* up.

The true Shop Rat will dodge the question. "I'm just chillin' till I go to Stratton for the Open,"† he might utter.

---

* Jack Daniel's and Coca-Cola. A favorite eye-opener for the *Singleplankus r. shopraticus.*

† The U.S. Open of snowboarding, which is held annually at Stratton Mountain, Vermont. Although thousands of North American Snowboarders claim they're headed for "the Open" very few actually make the pilgrimage.

"On my way to Vegas for the Show"* is another *Singleplankus r. shopraticus* deception.

He might even say: "Actually, I'm in the doctoral program at Yale.† Just waiting for my thesis to be published."

In the same way an actor in New York will never admit that he's a waiter, the *Singleplankus r. shopraticus* will consistently deny his own existence. Some have even been known to say: "I'm not in right now. Come back when someone is."

---

* A reference to the Las Vegas Snow Show. Since Vegas has the added draw of many strip bars, far more North American Snowboarders find their way to "Sin City."
† An East Coast college that has a strict anti-Snowboarder admittance policy.

This despite the fact that you can see the Coke stains on his shirtfront, see the space he's taking up on the workbench, and even smell his burning lip flesh (from the cigarette).

Once you have spotted the *Singleplankus r. shopraticus,* mark the appropriate box in your North American Snowboard Spotter Checklist (see p. 183), then turn and run from the shop immediately. Under no circumstances let this nonentity work on your snowboard or it too will end up in the *Singleplankus r. shopraticus*'s nonexistent parallel universe.

CHAPTER 7

Subspecies: Tourist

(Singleplankus r. rentalnightmaris)

The most common subspecies of *Singleplankus ripthehillicus* is the *Singleplankus r. rentalnight-maris,* also known as the North American Snowboarder Tourist.

Characterized by peeling, sunburned faces, boots worn on the wrong feet, jackets emblazoned with Denver Broncos or New York Jets logos, and rental snowboards bearing numbered stickers reading "Stem Christie Sports," the *Singleplankus r. rentalnightmarii* are at the bottom of the Snowboarder food chain.

As such, this subspecies makes it possible for all other species of *Singleplankus ripthehillicus* to

survive. For every day the North American Snowboard Tourist infuses the lifeblood of mountain resorts with pure, sweet cash flow. The wonderful thing about the Tourist is it doesn't mind spending like a drunken sailor. For the *Singleplankus r. rentalnightmaris* knows when it's doing its job. Shelling out ridiculous sums makes the normally city- and suburb-bound Tourist feel completely in balance with nature.

It's a lot like the gray whale.

Barnacles and lichen cling to the great whale as it swims through the ocean. Feeding off the current-borne crumbs that fall from the whale's massive mouth, and riding for free on its back, these parasites would flounder aimlessly and die without the whale. Yet the whale lumbers on, unfettered by the freeloaders.

The barnacle is to the gray whale what the Snowboarder is to the Tourist.

Whether the barnacle feels animosity toward the whale is largely unknown, but it is known that all other species of North American Snowboarder resent the Snowboarder Tourist. Each species displays this disdain in its own abusive way.

Strangely, the Tourist enjoys the abuse.

In the way you can tell how much a New Yorker likes you by the degree to which he/she argues with you, the Tourist gauges its worth by the amount of flak it takes.

Were it not slammed onto hard-packed snow by the Instructor, railroaded by the Carver, verbally abused and ignored by the Shop Rat, and bonked by the Jibber, the Tourist would feel utterly defeated. It is masochistic in its desire to be dissed.

Hailing from thickly populated, low-lying areas of the continent, the *Singleplankus r. rentalnightmaris* also feels a deep need to be surrounded by other humanoids. The closer the better.

This explains why the *Singleplankus r. rentalnightmaris* ritually rides trails that are the most crowded, feeds when every other Tourist on the mountain is feeding (causing massive crowds at midmountain restaurants), and comes to the hills only during their most crowded times.

Were it to come to the mountains and be left completely alone, not abused at all, it would suffer a complete nervous breakdown and most likely beach itself, like the great gray whale, on the massive sandbar of depression.

CHAPTER 8

Subspecies: Pro Bro

(Singleplankus r. paidforplayicus)

The highest rung in Snowboarder society is held by *Singleplankus r. paidforplayicus,* also known as the North American Pro Bro.* This species is usually descendant from either the Carver or the Jibber, although in very rare circumstances it might hail from Tourist, Shop Rat, or Instructor roots.

As its Latin name implies, the main characteristic that sets the Pro Bro apart is it gets paid to ride a Snowboard.

---

* This can as easily be a Board Betty as a Bro, but for purposes of alliteration and rhyme, I'll use Bro.

THANK YOU

In order to become a *Singleplankus r. paid-forplayicus,* the Snowboarder must work its way— through competition or frequent footing of the bill at late-night saloon gather- ings—up to a position of esteem within the Snow- boarder world. This position is often accompanied by a title (World Champion, Na- tional Champion, Bar Fix- ture). Once the Snowboarder has achieved some measure of success, it will travel to the Snow Show in Las Vegas (see Chapter 6). After chanting the aspiring Pro Bro's mantra ("Dude, can ya hook me?") several thousand times, the *Singleplankus r. paidforplayicus* wanna-be will find a company that will pay it to use its prod- ucts.* The Pro Bro will then don the badge that

---

* However, companies that make Gator bars or Zima will not re- quire the Snowboarder ever to ingest its products.

distinguishes the subspecies: the sponsorship patch. At this point, the Pro Bro will also decorate its vehicle with stickers bearing its sponsor's logo.

From that day on, the Pro Bro may be spotted riding in the halfpipe, a race course, in extreme* or boardercross† competitions, or on some of the world's most remote and pristine mountains.

On the last, the *Singleplankus r. paidforplayicus* will be participating in a high-level Snowboarder ritual known as the Photo Shoot. This is an activity in which the Pro Bro travels to the most unlikely destination possible, transported (often by helicopter) to the top of a peak, then with cameras trained on him, snowboards down, doing

Danger

everything he can to ignore the cameras and keep from smiling.‡

---

* Competitions in which Snowboarders vie to take the most dangerous line through insanely steep terrain, catch the most air off cliffs, and look the most calm while trying to keep from peeing their pants.

† A thrilling event in which six riders compete in a snowboard park. First one to the bottom wins. No rules. Part downhill, part roller derby.

‡ Unlike in cheesy ski magazines, smiling Snowboarders are strictly verboten in snowboard magazines, films, and especially posters. This is very serious business.

Not only will the Pro Bro be paid to perform this act of ignorance but his sponsors* will foot all his expenses.

Some Pro Bros do nothing but travel all over the world to ignore cameras. They no longer compete in their stated discipline (racing, half-pipe, sponsor butt-kissing) and have ascended to the heady realm of the Freerider.

In an amusing Snowboarder paradox, the Freerider never, ever, rides for free. It rides only when it gets paid to. The Freerider either is a fantastic rider or has a bro who heads the marketing department at a sunglasses or snowboard company. In this case the Freerider is paid to create an image that bespeaks complete indifference to the beautiful scenery or awe-inspiring mountains where it is filmed.

The final irony of the existence of both the Pro Bro and and the Freerider is that when their images appear in magazines and films (looking uninterested, blasé, and often constipated), they are

---

* Companies that have marketing departments run by Snowboarders who try to bankrupt the firms by paying their bros exorbitant sums to ride snowboards.

completely ignored by the snowboarding public. For along with the brutal hazing ceremony known as Snowboard Lesson No. 2, all aspiring Snowboarders learn to nonchalantly snub the whole world, including Pro Bros and Freeriders.

BOOK II

Behavior
of the
Snowboarder

CHAPTER 9

Grooming Habits of the Snowboarder

There is a widely held misconception that the North American Snowboarder does not groom.

Sure, his clothes dangle off him like limp dishrags, he allows errant hummocks of nubby hair to sprout on his face like weeds, and he seems to have lost the bag containing all his toiletries, but for all his disheveled nonchalance in the personal grooming department, the *Singleplankus ripthehillicus* is a strictly groomed creature.

Of course the North American Snowboarder looks like a slob, but he *means* to look this way. Slobs, by contrast, have wound up willy-nilly at their slovenly states.

Yes, it just takes a trained eye to recognize the effort. Consider the Snowboarder's hair. You think that oily rock-star look just happens? Whoa no.

The Snowboarder harvests grease, then adds it to his locks. Don't believe me? Chart the annual dollar figures for sales of snowboards. Now overlay the sales of STP motor oil. It's no coincidence that Snowboarder gatherings smell like an Indy pit.

Another Snowboarder coiffure trick is bleaching out his hair. This can be done neither professionally nor totally. Beneath the white, heavily damaged hair, at least one half inch of dark roots must be visible. The Board Bro has been known to tape the roots of his hair (in the same way one would tape a window before painting a house) before applying bleach.

The well-groomed Snowboarder always straddles the muddy line between disheveled or dirty and outright repulsiveness. Facial hair can grow freely, like wheat on the prairie, but nose hair must not so much as poke from nostril caves. Goatees and sideburns are all the rage; ear hair must be snipped or dug out (yet another use for the ever-popular multifaceted snowboard tool). Grease- or P-tex-caked fingernails are as desirable to the Snowboarder as Lee Clip-on Nails and pink Cadillacs are to the Mary Kay cosmetologist. Yet toe cheese is to the Snowboarder what 7-Eleven burritos are to Julia Child.*

It's not that dirt and collections of bodily secretions are verboten; they just must be displayed in a particularly Snowboarderly way. Sure, it's nebulous and paradoxical,† but who said being a Snowboarder was easy?

The credo here, for those who desire to slip into the fold, is to look like you just fixed the tractor and plowed the fields, smell like you cleaned the stables, but never show the slightest sign that you've glanced in a mirror.

---

* A woman chef who became famous for being able to make an onion cry with the shrill tone of her voice.
† I don't know what these words mean either. I just put them in so my parents (long in hiding over the shame of their son becoming a Snowboarder) might read them and feel that they didn't waste all that money on college.

THE SNOWBOARDER'S MEDICINE CABINET
- Hair bleach
- A & D ointment (for new tattoos)
- 1,000-count bottle of ibuprofen (for pain of sprains and fractures)
- Nail polish (Board Bro only)
- Condoms (Board Betty only)
- Nose rings and cheek studs (discarded for bigger ones)
- One unused razor
- Battery-operated nose-hair trimmer
- Snowboard multipurpose tool

What's the difference between a vacuum cleaner and a snowboard?

The way you attach the dirt bag.

CHAPTER 10

Feeding Habits
of the Snowboarder

The blue whale can eat 4 tons of shrimplike animals called krill in one day. Its infants routinely gain as much as 200 pounds every twenty-four hours.

While not on a scale with the blue whale, the North American Snowboarder is nonetheless a ravenous eater. The feeding grounds for the *Singleplankus ripthehillicus* may vary, but one characteristic will always be the same: The Snowboarder will always eat where food is cheap or free.

For this reason all-you-can-eat buffets* are enough to send the North American Snowboarder into a feeding frenzy. Here it can mow down enough grub to distend its stomach. Yet buffets are good for much more than one big meal. Thanks to its excessively baggy attire, the Snowboarder can conceal and pilfer enough pies, sandwiches, and biscuits (sometimes with gravy) to keep itself and a bro or two fed for a week or more.

Snowboarders are also known to frequent Asian restaurants around midday. The word has gone out over the Snowboarder network that these restaurants often have major lunch specials. And Snowboarders like moo goo gai pan. There's nothing special about the dish; they just like saying "moo goo."

The Snowboarder also feeds at its work site. This is especially handy for Snowboarders who work in restaurants, less so for those employed in T-shirt shops (although Hanes Beefy T-shirts have been known to sustain Snowboarders for long periods between feedings).[†]

---

* Las Vegas's Circus Circus—the Mac Daddy of all buffets—is an annual gathering spot during the Snow Show.
[†] It is a genetic fact that Snowboarders have stomachs like billy goats'.

Vigilant Snowboard spotters will also find Snowboarders feeding in supermarkets. Bulk food bins offer amazing grazing opportunities. Here, however, the Snowboarder must be crafty. Predators (in-store detectives, overzealous sales-clerks) must always be watched for (technically, grazing is illegal). This, however, makes grazing that much more appealing for the Snowboarder. A chocolate-covered pretzel served with larceny sauce is just so much tastier than one that was actually paid for.

Many Snowboarders can also be found feeding at 7-Eleven stores during the late-night or early-morning hours. Here they will swarm the microwave oven. When a beep issues, the Snowboarders will attack like a pack of hyenas and devour soft and helpless burritos.

When the Snowboarder does not have the energy to go out and forage for its food, it will, as a last resort, order it from Domino's. Once at the home of the Snowboarder, the Domino's delivery-man will be faced with all manner of scams to part him from his pizza without the ponying up of any cash. By the time the Domino's man gives up trying to collect any money or is forced from the house by the threat of being stabbed by a snowboard tool, the pizza will be cold and the beer warm.

This does not matter to the North American Snowboarder. In its prime it can down seventeen slices of pizza and gain as much as twenty pounds in one sitting. While this is insignificant compared with the intake of the blue whale, it should be noted that the blue whale is the size of thirty elephants. The Snowboarder is far smaller than even one elephant, although its pants would fit Dumbo just fine.

CHAPTER 11

Courtship and Mating Rituals of the Snowboarder

A male lion can perform sexual intercourse as many as 150 times in a forty-eight-hour period. One especially popular species of tropical bat can hang twice its body weight from its tongue. The penis of a gray whale is 7 feet long.

Next to these impressive facts, the sexual equipment and appetites of the Snowboarder look puny and pathetic. Or maybe not. Let's see that gray whale do it in a gondola. That studly male lion may be able to shred the torso of a gazelle in seconds, but can he unhook a black vinyl push-up brassiere from under a tight-fitting retro sweater?

I don't think so.

And what about Mr. Tongue Bat? Let's see. The dude can launch really big air and please his mate at the same time.

Okay, he rules.

While not able to perform this kind of feat, at least not without a safety net, the Snowboarder has mating habits that are nonetheless quite bizarre.

First there is the courtship ritual. The initial stage of this ancient dance, which dates way back to before Prince* was the Artist Formerly Known as Prince, is performed in or around a halfpipe or snowboard park. These structures, although supposedly constructed for recreation, were actually fabricated as the prime regions of courtship for Snowboarders.

Consider the shape of the halfpipe. Its vast concavity invites the Snowboarder into its midst, enveloping him as he shoots in and out. The better the wax and the more skilled the rider, the farther out the Snowboarder can fly—thereby "reentering" with greater thrust.

---

* A small-framed singer with an ego so massive it couldn't be contained in a simple name.

Consider also the terminology of the pipe. One "goes down the tube," "works the lips," and "bones it out." The "flat bottom" of the pipe is to be pushed into repeatedly as the Snowboarder readies himself to poke his board out, then slide back in. A good rider is said to be "going off" in the pipe.

You don't need to be Freud.*

Then there is the snowboard park. Great breastlike hummocks adorn the "flat belly" of the park. Curved "hips" rise up. The experienced boarder barely caresses these on his way to the ultimate goal: the big air. Located just below the center of the park, the big air is where a Snowboarder can really perform his stuff.

The female of the Snowboarder species will study male riders as they work the pipe. Watching to learn how to boost out? Not even.

The male's pipe riding is the greatest clue that the female will get as to how he stacks up as a mate. Does he charge in too fast? Blow all his energy on the first hit? Does he ride in tentatively

---

* The father of all psychoanalysts, who predicted the behavior of Snowboarders when he said, "Sex is the driving force behind all actions."

and too slow? Fail to get off as he goes down the pipe?

Much as the female of the species Disco Dancer (*Loungelizardus maximus*) studies the opposite gender on the dance floor, the female Snowboarder will watch for performance in the pipe as an indication of sexual prowess.

After spotting her prospective mate, the female Snowboarder makes herself available. She accomplishes this by positioning herself at the top of the pipe. Next, she'll take to fiddling with her high-back bindings until her selected mate arrives.

The male of the species generally blows it at this point.

In an effort to show her more of his stuff, he'll usually zoom right past her, only to be befuddled when, after ripping a monster pipe run, he turns to find she's gone off with a sensitive snowboard instructor of the nineties.

Of course, the male doesn't know that the female has seen enough by the time she positions herself at the mouth of the pipe. If the male pays more attention to pipe at this point, the female will construe this as competition.

If, however, the male shows interest, the female will ride with him. During their first ride together, the male will always lead. As the male is still not sure he has been picked, he will unnecessarily use their first run together to further demonstrate his riding techniques (which we've already established are seen as indicating his sexual proficiency).

At this point, the male's display is redundant and may demonstrate to the female that he will not ever pay her much attention. If the male so much as glances back to see how the female is doing, however, she will take this as encouragement and move the courtship to its next stage: the chairlift.

The way a courting Snowboarder couple loads a chairlift is of utmost importance. If the female is interested in the male, she will position herself so that, once on the lift, her board will have to cross and touch his.

Goofy-footed riders hang to the right, and regular-footed riders hang left. This crossing of boards is accomplished by placing a goofy-footed rider on the left of a regular footer.

Since the male is trying to strike a good pose (casually indifferent to all around him while checking his goatee in the sunglasses of the ticket checker), he is oblivious to the female's lift-line maneuvers. This makes it easier for the female to

shimmy into position. As they sit down next to each other, and the chair swings past the ramp, the male is put on alert as soon as her board touches his.

A male in this stage is enjoyable to watch. As soon as he senses something touching his board, the male Snowboarder will tense and ready himself for a fight. This reaction has caused many a male to twitch right off the chairlift. Some have even fallen to their death.* It is for this reason that some states, such as the snowboard habitat

---

* This bit of hyperbole is an example of why one should never let a Snowboarder near a word processor, much less a publisher.

of Vermont, have instituted chairlift safety bar laws.

If the male can keep from spazzing his way off the chairlift, and hold his punch for long enough, he may look over and see that he is seated next to a comely boardess. At this point he may actually smile, revealing to her for the first time his pierced tongue.

After the first crossing on the chairlift, the courting Snowboarder couple can move past the halfpipe. At this stage the male may take the next step by showing the female his secret stash. This is generally some little known grotto in the trees where the powder stays freshest the longest. Again, you don't have to be Freud to register the significance of a hidden "virgin" powder run.

Once the male has shown the female his secret stash, he will generally plunge in first and savor the tastiest line for himself, leaving her to forage for scraps. This is the second time the female Snowboarder considers exiting the courtship.

The male, meanwhile, is oblivious to her considerations. He's just let her ride his stash, how much more could he do?

If the courtship somehow continues, the Snowboarder couple will find themselves moving toward consummation. Depending on the religious-moral convictions of the Snowboarders involved, this may take anywhere from two to seven runs down the mountain.

The consummation ceremony goes like this. They walk over to the gondola together, the male all swagger, the female bouncing (see Chapter 23 for more on the Snowboarder's walk) up to the ticket checker. The male allows the female to flash her season pass first. He then follows her down the aisle toward the gondola.

Once at the front of the line, the female waits for just the right car. Then the male creates some sort of diversion that will ensure they are the only two in the car (chomping on a large, New Jersey–grown cigar will generally do the trick).

Nothing happens until the gondola car leaves the terminal. Once they are out, the male reaches into his pants and pulls it out. The female Snowboarder takes hold of it. His snowboard wax, that is. She then spreads a generous amount onto her snowboard. The male then takes his snowboard and rubs it against hers until they can't tell where her wax ends and his begins.

As the car pulls into the top terminal, the newly consummated Snowboarder couple emerge with shiny boards and a general aura of deep satisfaction. This couple, in the eyes of the great gods of Snowboarders, are now fastened together like a high-back to a Jibber's deck.

What do you call a Snowboarder who's just broken up with his girlfriend?
Homeless.

And while he has not exhibited the enormity of the gray whale or the insatiability of the lion, or even the high-flying tricks of the tropical bat, the male Snowboarder has a faster stick as a result of the union.

A NOTE FOR SNOWBOARD SPOTTERS

You can tell married and long-term-relationship Snowboarder couples from courting couples either by the way their boards hang parallel from the chairlift or by their insistence on reading snowboard magazines in the gondola.

POP QUIZ

1. While peeing in the woods behind the halfpipe, you find a strange bottle. You pick it up and rub it so you can see what label (you want to know if it's a cool brand—Mountain Dew, or Molson Ice, or any other product that advertises by using Snowboarders) is under the grime. A genie pops out and gives you one wish. You wish for:
   a. World peace.
   b. A million dollars.
   c. Just one night with the Board Betty/Bro who just boned out a sweet method in the pipe.

2. You've just realized that you've fallen in love with the mate of your dreams. You tell him/her by going to:
   a. A fancy restaurant and, over a bottle of champagne, pledging your undying love.
   b. The top of your favorite mountain, and in front of all your buds, screaming out your eternal love.
   c. The top of a virgin powder field and letting him/her poach your favorite line.

3. Your would-be mate has agreed to spend the rest of his/her life with you. You:
   a. Buy a ring.
   b. Reserve a chapel.
   c. Pierce your belly button. Engrave a small snowboard pendant with his/her name. Hang it off a chain like a stainless steel umbilical cord.

4. Your newly betrothed takes you to a religious service with his/her deeply religious family. After flailing through the rites of the church/temple/mosque, and faced with a family who clearly think your tattoos and green hair equate you to the Antichrist, you:
   a. Get down on your knees and repent.
   b. Offer alms for the collection box.
   c. Tell the joke in which God thinks he's a Vail snowboard instructor.

If you picked answer *c* for every question, you are a Snowboarder. If you knew the joke in which God thinks he's a Vail snowboard instructor, call me. I'll cast you in the movie version of this book.

CHAPTER 12

Plumage of the Snowboarder

The North American cardinal, a stellar and largely Republican bird, has developed a striking plumage differentiation between the sexes. The male wears a coat of red that is so brilliant it could only blend in at baseball stadiums in Cincinnati or St. Louis, or possibly at a New England links-style golf course. The female is decked out in far less showy hues and can hide anywhere except an Audubon calendar.*

* A beige and brown wildlifey version of *Where's Waldo?*

While some might think nature has slighted the female by giving her the shabby dress, it's actually quite the opposite. With its sartorial red-headed splendor, nature has duped the male into thinking he's special. Really it's just made him predator bait. Not only does this account for the short life span of the nonchildbearing cardinal but it's just one more argument that nature is indeed a woman, and clearly a real mother.

Unlike the cardinal, the North American Snowboarder's plumage is exactly the same in the male and female. Loose-fitting and smocklike, Snowboarder plumage cloaks sex. All the bumps and bulges by which *Homo sapiens* happily identify the sex of their species are effectively smoothed over, tucked away in the bread box of anonymity.

Each and every outer garment the Snowboarder wears must hang like drapery. This harkens back to the origins of the *Singleplankus ripthehillicus*. In the early days the Snowboarder roosted in the trees near mountain resorts. When the first light would hit its one-man pup tent, the Snowboarder would rise, wrapping the tent around itself, grab its board, and ride. Thus the initial "look" of the Snowboarder was equated with an ill-fitting, flapping tent.

When Big-Time Manufacturers got into the act, they simply measured the way a tent fit and mass-produced the suckers. Then they marketed the canopy-cut garments by claiming they offered "greater ease of movement." Since there had also been a great decrease in the number of circus clowns employed in North America, those same Big-Time Manufacturers had something of a glut of clown pants stashed in hundreds of warehouses. The baggy look played right into their hands.

There is only one garment that the North American Snowboarder wears tight: the knit "beanie" cap. It uniformly wears this pulled down to its eyebrows, and often over its eyes (when trying to be coy). This mandatory cap is never to be taken off in public.

Of course, this further confuses the gender of the North American Snowboarder. Let this be a warning to those foolhardy non-Snowboarders who would venture into a Snowboarder keg party in search of a mate. You may not know what you're getting until it's way too late.

Such gender cloaking means the childbearing female of the species is just as likely to be attacked by predators (cranky ski patrollers or pesky rent-a-cops) as the male. Many take this as a sign that Mother Nature is not eager to perpetuate this species.

Although gender cannot be discerned by the Snowboarder's plumage, the stages of Snowboarder development can be.

In its larva or Newrider stage, the Snowboarder can be identified by baggy, styleless plaids and hooded sweatshirts. Cotton is to the early Snowboarder what lip fuzz is to the pubescent boy. At this stage, the Newrider's coat will be dark, most commonly brown. This is why many Newrider Snowboarders are mistaken for United Parcel Service deliverymen.

As the Snowboarder matures, however, its cloak molts, the cotton (a victim of considerable mold) falls away like lizard skin. It is then replaced by stiffer, more resilient fabrics whose names begin with important-looking capital letters (Gore-Tex, Thinsulate, Windstopper).*

At this stage the Snowboarder also thinks itself extremely Important. This sophomoric phase (you can always tell a sophomore, but not much)

---

* Trademarked names for overteched nylon.

is known as the Realrider stage. At this stage, the Snowboarder will assume perches (on barstools or chairlifts) from which it will trap and bedazzle others with its quintessential knowledge of life as taken from *Zen and the Art of Snowboarding.*

(This book has actually never been written, principally because it would be redundant. For, in the same way a virgin male *Homo sapiens* will pretend he knows everything there is to know about sex, virtually every Snowboarder thinks a thorough understanding of Zen came with its first pair of Airwalks.)

I was recently cornered by a twenty-one-year-old Realrider on a rickety chairlift in Wyoming.* When the chairlift stopped in midair, the Realrider had me cornered. "See, dude, you're probably not going to get this because, where do you live, New York?"

"Vail, Colorado," I told him.

"Right, so you won't get this because you don't live in the mountains. But we're seated in the youngest mountain range in the U.S. That means it's full of energy. I seat myself in these higher temples so I can conduct myself with that

* A state where they inexplicably call huge hills "holes."

energy and become ooooh so rich. It's a different kind of wealth, not monetary."

"And that sponsor patch on your jacket is . . . ?"

" 'Cause they pay me good money to wear it," he said with pride.

I let it slide.

"Snowboarding has taught me so much about life and the duality of forces," he yammered. "In religion there's God and Satan, in a battery it's positive and negative. Right, like one on each end?"

Stuck in a chairlift with Buddha Realrider, I nodded numbly.

"In our quest to find ourselves within these forces, it's not up to us to control. It's up to us to stay balanced. If you look at a C-shaped carve, that's the yin and yang in life."

The chairlift still wasn't moving.

"What the hell's wrong with this chair?" I yelled.

He let out a Big Sigh, obviously thinking: This guy's just not getting it.

"Dude, you gotta Zen out. See, your run down the mountain is you flowing through life—"

At this point I jumped off the chairlift. I know it was cowardly, but I was desperate, and a broken tibia is a small price to pay for a healthy headful of non-Zen neurosis.

Sunburned nostrils (from riding with their noses turned up) are telling characteristics of Realrider Snowboarders. Broken noses and black eyes are also common traits. As their gazes are perpetually focused on the sky instead of the ground, Realriders are susceptible to many slope-side mishaps (slamming into trees or unsuspecting skiers, getting their yin caught in their yang). Tragically, many suffer consequences more dire than a simple broken nose and never move past this stage of development.

The ones that do survive Realrider-dom become Pro Bro Snowboarders. They are the most advanced and interesting of the Snowboarder species. As the name implies, these are riders who get paid (even if with just a free rubber vomit stomp pad) to ride.

While the ambiguity of the Pro Bro is great—one might be a world champion while another may get beer money to hang at the pipe—its plumage will be largely the same. Its hair inexplicably turns a yellow-white color that's not normally found in nature. Next its mop will change from green to orange to striped to fire engine red—often in the short span of a week.

Lately the Pro Bro, influenced by a secret plot hatched in the corporate offices of Hemmy Hagar,[*] has also taken a shine to all things seventies. Glam is replacing grunge in the plumage of the Pro Bro Snowboarder. All garments that hearken back to the 1970s, whether vinyl, polyester, or Formica, are widely coveted by the Pro Bro. This explains the many nocturnal sightings of Wayne Newton[†] look-alikes in places like Lake Tahoe, California.

Of course, whatever the Pro Bro dons instantly becomes the uniform of Wanna-bes and Neverwills. These two lesser strains of the North American Snowboarder species are identifiable by one and only one trademark: They're the ones wearing the sponsor patches.

In the future, evidence of the Pro Bro's ironic revisionism (in magazine photos and snowboard films) will be the bane of many a Snowboarder's existence. In ten years, when they are no longer Pro Bros and living by the irrefutable and pecu-

---

[*] A little-known polyester tycoon.
[†] The crooning king of polyester.

liar Glory Days Time Construct (the older I get, the better I was), the Pro Bro will rue the day it ever rode in a faux gold Formica jacket meant to look like your mom's kitchen table.

But that's someday.

For now, it's way better to look like Danny Bonaduce* than a North American cardinal.

Rad Snowboarder Clothing Brands
- Stuff
- Swag
- Porn Star†
- Fuct‡

---

* The hip-hugger-wearing, redheaded singer in the Partridge Family, last seen peddling suede bell-bottoms on infomercials.
† Should be worn only by those with divine endowment, if you know what I mean.
‡ The telephone receptionist at this company must sound like a real gutter rat: "Hello, this is Fuct."

CHAPTER 13

Ornamentation of the Snowboarder

Members of the human species crave that which they do not have. The male human, being too brutish to decorate a living room with anything more elaborate than lawn chairs and beer crates, pursues the softer sensibility of the female. In a fervent desire to endow simple household items* with major symbolic importance, the female *Homo sapiens* is likewise attracted to the presence of the male.

As the North American Snowboarder is (arguably) a subspecies of *Homo sapiens,* it is also drawn to that which it does not have: sharpness.

* Such as the toilet seat.

The Snowboarder lives in a soft world. The snow is soft (except in the case of the East Coast Snowboarder, whose head is soft from repeated confrontations with the hard, icy snow); snowboards are rounded; attitudes and mores are spongy; pointy fingers are snapped, swollen, and covered with heavy, rounded mittens. Virtually every facet of the Snowboarder's world is buffered and blunted.

Thus the Snowboarder lusts after pointiness.

This is why it ritually subjects itself to penetration from sharp objects in its elaborate ornamentation rituals. By punching holes into its soft tissue (with needles, guns, or the ever-handy Snowboarder's multitool), the Snowboarder satisfies its want for sharpness while creating a cavity that can be filled with a metallic cultural icon (a grommet or Cadillac hood ornament) meant to convey a message to other members of the tribe.

For what is a nose ring if not the Snowboarder's version of the college tie?* Indeed the Snowboarder's tongue stud is nothing more than

---

* A dated reference to a fabric loop worn around the neck that indicated a man had attended an Ivy League college. It has since been replaced with a rope.

its American Express into the caste of Snow-boarder society.*

Where the Snowboarder elects to lacerate its flesh dictates its level in the caste. Earlobes and eyebrows are okay for newbies, but the dedicated Snowboarder prefers to make Swiss cheese out of much softer tissue (cheeks, belly buttons, scro-tums).

The message this sends to peer group Snow-boarders: I'm the real thing.

If that message doesn't come through via vari-ous totems, the Snowboarder will actually have it written into its skin in tattoo ink.

This has prompted Coca-Cola to file copyright infringement suits against scads of Snowboarders who have emblazoned the company's slogan across their backs, up their inner thighs, and around their necks.

As with piercings, tattoos titillate the Snow-boarder with a thousand needle pricks. Getting a tattoo is to the Snowboarder what scorching himself on that burning hibachi at the beginning of *Kung Fu* was to Kwai Chang Caine.† With the

* "Membership has its privileges."
† David Carradine's ass-kicking character in the best TV show of all time.

same fear and relish that Kwai Chang burned his flesh, the Snowboarder will sidle up to the tattooist's needle.

Many would argue that the Snowboarder, by subjecting itself to so much pain, is doing penance for something it feels guilty about (like spending its days sliding down a snow-covered mountain instead of doing more adult things, such as chasing small numbers up and down a big stock market). Freudians would also have a

field day with the Snowboarder's propensity for being poked and prodded.

Yet those who closely study the North American Snowboarder know it scars and defaces its body simply because it thinks it looks bitchin'.

Of course, if tattoos and pierced flesh were the only measure of a Snowboarder's bitchin'-ness, Dennis Rodman would be the happenin'-est 'boarder around.

Fortunately for ski patrols, neither Rodman nor Kwai Chang ever hooked a deal with Burton.

CHAPTER 14

Symbols of the Snowboard Culture

From Plato's cave to Freud's interpretation of a sword to the sexual connotation of green M & M's,* symbols reflect a culture's thoughts and beliefs. The snowboard culture is especially rife with symbols, yet they are not all what they seem.

When stalking the symbols of the snowboard culture it is essential to arm oneself with the sharp stick of irony. By irony I mean not only the juxtaposition of unlikely images or ideas that create a smirk, but the ability to see that the emperor indeed wears no clothes while still deeming

---

* If you have to ask, you're not old enough to know.

that nakedness cool. For most symbols of the snowboard culture count on their viewer to be "in on the joke." The joke is generally a tongue-in-cheek re-representation of pop culture. To understand it, and to smirk knowingly, is not to be amused; it is to gain admittance to the cult.

A jacket emblazoned with a small breast-pocket design (a red star or a yellow shell) that looks like one worn by a pump jockey in a gas station out of *The Great Gatsby* is a popular

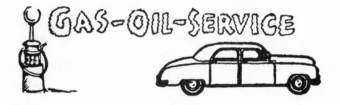

symbol. In the past the jacket indicated that its wearer worked for Texaco or Shell. Today it's worn mostly to piss off parents who really don't want their sons or daughters to look like they wipe dipsticks.

A peace sign does not mean, "no war," as it did in the 1960s and '70s. Rather it means, "I am hip and retro and have no idea what 'no war' means since that's all I've ever known."

Double entendres of a sexual nature are also

popular with the Snowboarder. The least clever, thereby offering the maximum affront to the sensibilities of the staid and stuffy, the better. Ride snowboards, for example, offers not business cards but condoms printed with its name (on the wrapper—there is a limit, even for Snowboarders). "Ride Condom," the wrapper reads, "so they can't see ya coming."

While printed condoms may not be as allegorical as Plato's cave or as metaphorical as Freud's sword, they can be used to penetrate much more than symbolic truths. And let's face it, the North American Snowboarder is much more inclined to chomp green M & M's than to chew on a tome of Freudian theory or Platonic platitudes.*

* No, I don't know what this means either. Sure sounds swell, though, doesn't it?

CHAPTER 15

Popular Art of the Snowboard Culture

An artist named Marianne Magne draws, scratches, paints, incinerates, and lacerates. And that's just putting on her makeup.

No, really, this is how Mademoiselle Magne creates her art. Her images are scarred and damaged. Her colors are dark and frequently display bloodred wounds. She is very popular with the North American Snowboarder.

Why?

Because the soul of the North American Snowboarder is more interested in destruction and defacement than in creation and a pretty face. Harsh, you say? Well, one need only look at the vocabulary the Snowboarder uses to describe a pleasant experience.

Someone who "ripped a phat line" rode down the hill nicely. A "nose poke" is a fun jump. To say a 'boarder "shredded" is to pay him/her the ultimate compliment. (Superlatives being easier than thoughtful metaphors, this term has become hackneyed and decidedly unhip in today's Snowboarder world.)

Yes, the soul of the Snowboarder is angry and destructive. Consider Snowboarder music. Will you ever hear Julie Andrews* crooning "The hills

* An actress who once played a nanny in a film called *The Sound of Music*. The plotline, which involves the escape of a bunch of innocent folks from the clutches of the Nazis, is quite instructional for Snowboarders looking to outwit ski patrollers.

are alive with the sound of music" at a Snowboarder party? Not unless it's an acid house
remix or is being played by a thrash band called
Poison or Nail or Fungus* (band's names must
have dark, violent, or grotty connotations).

Likewise there are certain rules for Snowboarder music. The most important is the strict
prohibition of rhythm or melody. Snowboarder
music needs to be raspy, fuzzy, harsh. It is only
with a growling rasp that the Snowboarder can
meld its soul to the music.

Go to a Snowboarder concert. If there is a single tapping foot, it will be attached to someone
who has downed one too many Jolt colas.† For
there is nothing to tap to. Growling guitars and
suicidal rantings are what crank the Snowboarder's organs.

Is this a negative? Far from it. For in today's
world it means the Snowboarder can find music
just about anywhere. Where there is sound and
huge amplification, a happy Snowboarder will be

---

* These are either actual band names or what a Snowboarder sees
when he takes off his socks.
† A heavily caffeinated brand of soda that gives you what its name
promises. As such, it could not have been developed by anyone on
Madison Avenue.

found. This explains why so many Snowboarders take jobs as dishwashers. The Snowboarder listens to the gush, gurgle, and roar of the Hobart* the way a piano teacher would lend a scholarly ear to Chopin.†

Snowboarders have also been know to flock to basement boiler rooms in the large hotels where they work. Many thought this was so they could be in a clandestine location for inhalation of certain controlled and flammable substances, but that's not the reason at all.

For the Snowboarder, the ghastly roar in a boiler room is better than Beck, cheaper than a Chili Peppers disc. Also, the oily air in boiler rooms helps the Snowboarder maintain the 10W40 viscosity in its hair.

So, if a culture's art is representative of the collective unconscious of its members, does this mean the soul of the Snowboarder is primarily violent? Maybe, but don't tell a Snowboarder that—unless you want your tires slashed.

---

* The most commonly found brand of dishwashing machine. The brand name is also used in the job-experience slot on the résumés of ex-Snowboarders in the form "Hobart Engineer."
† An ancient European John Tesh kind of dude.

CLASSIC SNOWBOARDER FILMS
- *Dazed and Confused*
- *Scarface*
- *Shaft*
- *Fast Times at Ridgemont High*
- *Repo Man*
- *Heavy Metal*
- *Star Wars*
- Any Japanimation films

SNOWBOARDER'S MUST-READ LIST
- *On the Road*
- *Fear and Loathing in Las Vegas*
- *Blunt* magazine
- *Stick* magazine
- *TransWorld Snowboard* magazine
- *Snowboard Life* (for the aging Snowboarder)
- Any porno magazine
- This book

BOOK III

Where Did
the Snowboarder
Come From, and
Where Is He/She
Now?

CHAPTER 16

The Snowboard Creation Myth

The term "myth" was first coined by the Greek historian Herodotus in the fifth century B.C. He used it to distinguish what he saw as essentially fictional accounts of the past from factual description. Herodotus hoped that these fanciful stories, once labeled as lies, would disappear from human consciousness and that the "truth" would instead prevail. The old Greek did not, however, consider that humans usually prefer big lies to little truths. Lies tell so much more. Calling them myths makes them seem not quite so naughty.

So here, with no apology offered to Herodotus,

and honed by hundreds of fitful, alcohol-inspired retellings from one quarter-beer happy hour to the next, is the Snowboard Creation Myth.

High up in the Himalaya, in a time before Jesus, Confucius, and cell phones, there lived a tribe of mountain people known as the Boarderani. The Boarderani wore tight-fitting snow leopard skins and hats topped with rooster cowls. To get about the high, snowy peaks, they strapped a long plank to each foot. They called these skissers.

Each person in the clan was awarded, on his/her second birthday, a pair of skissers. Because the Boarderani lived high in the mountains, where there were no trees to fell for their skissers, they had to travel far down the mountainsides to get wood each year. Thus, skissers were very valuable indeed. As the tribe began to grow it became more and more difficult to make skissers for each new member.

The king of the Boarderani, Alberto, made a decree: Each couple would be allotted one pair of skissers for their offspring. In doing so, King Al instituted not only the first tree conservation program but also the world's first birth control policy. For the Boarderani it made no sense to have children if they couldn't give them skissers.

The only man in the tribe who didn't wear tight-fitting snow leopard clothes was Daffy, the jester. Famous for making the elders of the tribe laugh by jumping off the ground and running through the air with his skissers on, Daffy wore very baggy clothing to facilitate his stunts. He was an irresistible show-off, and as such he attracted the attention of the most fertile and desirable of the Boarderani women: Surfsuptua.

The two had a marvelous wedding, where much gluhwien was drunk, and on their wedding night they conceived a child. All the village rejoiced, and Daffy skissered off down the mountain to fell a tree for his child's skissers.

As fate would have it, that was an epic snow year in the Himalaya. We're talkin' megadumps. If the Boarderani had been a more thoughtful people, this would've been the year to first use snorkels in the snow.

But Daffy, the most inventive of the Boarderani, had his mind on other things. After noticing that the Boarderani with wider skissers were able to get around better in deep snow, and hoping to give his child every possible advantage, he made his child's skissers way fat.

By the time he got back, Surfsuptua was very pregnant. Her belly had grown to wondrous proportions. All the village waited for her child, knowing it would be huge and beautiful.

When the day came, Daffy and Surfsuptua set the village on its ear by giving birth not to one child but to twins—the first ever seen in the Himalaya.

The proud parents named the girl Tweakskea and the boy Bonkomano. Thing is, Daffy had only one pair of skissers for the two children. They sought special dispensation, but King Al would allow none. Not being able to choose between his two beautiful children, Daffy split the skissers. "Someday, when you are grown and able to make your own skissers, you will be far better at skissering for having ridden on only one all these years," he told them.

Daffy was not only a jester, he was the first spin doctor.

Tweakskea and Bonkomano began riding their skissers with both feet lashed to the same board. Gradually, the two of them adopted a more sideways stance. As Daffy was training both Tweak and Bonk to be jesters, they wore loose-fitting clothes like their father's. The baggies, in addition to having only one skisser to ride, alienated Tweak and Bonk from their peers.

They were the butt of jokes and jeers from all the other kids. Not only did the kids make fun of Tweak and Bonk but they also drew dozens of derogatory pictures of the two outcasts on the walls of the neighborhood cave.

As Tweak and Bonk grew, however, the jeers were less and less frequent. In the deep snow of the Himalaya, Tweak and Bonk ruled. The skisser kids flailed.

Soon the village was filled with extra single skissers as more and more of the happenin' kids began to ride sideways. This worried King Al; not only did all the new kids ride standing sideways in baggy clothes, but since the limited number of skissers had kept the population growth in check, the village was now in the throes of a full-blown sexual revolution. The birthrate doubled to fill the void.

King Al quickly banned single skissers from the village. Still the youngsters rode. A major fracture had occurred in the once peaceful hamlet. It might have led to insurrection if it weren't for Wank, a peer of Tweak and Bonk.

Wank was a weak rider, but he had a serious thing for Tweak. The dude, however, didn't stand a chance. Not only did Tweak disdain Wank but

Bonk wouldn't hear of his sister dating the weakling.

In an effort to prove himself to Tweak, Wank hiked above the town one day.

It was well known that skisser riders were not allowed to ride uphill of the village. Yet, as fate would have it, the most enticing extreme skissering lines existed above the village.

Wank dropped in on the most rad line that anyone in the village had ever attempted. Sure enough, two turns in, he augered.* He went over the bars and began to tumble. As he did, the mountain began to move with him. In seconds a small snowslide had metamorphosed into a major avalanche. The slide buried the town and everyone in it.

Bonk and Tweak, Daffy and Surfsuptua all perished. The only survivor was King Al, who'd been in Tibet visiting his mistress. As Al wasn't the brightest light (a product of royal inbreeding), he was unable to find where his village had once stood. Instead, he grabbed his mistress and began another kingdom in the Himalaya.

---

* To auger is to jam the board into the snow in a manner that causes the rider to be propelled ass over toes.

After seeing how single-skisser riding had led to a sexual revolution amongst his old subjects, the king kept it a secret from his new ones. Al dedicated the rest of his life to spreading the good word on two-plank skissering.

Al's skills as a public speaker left something to be desired, however. He had a very bad lisp. In due course his agent had King Al drop the "-ssering" from "skissering." Thus Al left us with the easy to pronounce word "ski."

Now one-plank skiing, or snowboarding, might have lain forever beneath a glacier in the Himalaya, if it hadn't been for Daffy. You see, before he died, Daffy wrote this story down on a pair of skissers. The story stayed there for two thousand years.

That was when a '60s throwback hippie from Vermont named Jed journeyed into the Himalaya to find himself. In his quest, he fell down a deep crevasse. He woke up in a cave with strange pictures of surferlike prehistoric people. And he found Daffy's skissers. After climbing out of the crevasse, Jed rode all the way back to Kathmandu on a fossilized skisser.

Back in Vermont, he showed these skissers to his buddy, Jake Burton Carpenter, then hit the road for Machu Picchu, where he had heard the self he was looking for might be lingering. Soon after Jed's exit, Jake began manufacturing skissers and putting his name on them.

Although he kept the history a secret, Jake did name a few of the tricks in the sport he helped invent after its progenitors: Tweak and Bonk. As for Wank, suffice to say he too was remembered, although not nearly as fondly.

CHAPTER 17

Evolution and the Snowboarder

Way back before the Boarderani, before Bonk and Tweak, the predecessors of today's North American Snowboarders walked on all fours.

These preboarder *Homo sapiens* went from walking on their hands and feet to a bipedal existence* for a number of reasons: A biped's free hands were able to gather food, erect posture offered less surface area to absorb the sun's heat, and they got much more wear out of their Levi's 501s.

The modern-day Snowboarder is putting evo-

---

* In which man stood upright on two feet. Of course, this was long before the invention of the couch, which changed all that.

lution into rewind. Whereas its forebears stood erect, the Snowboarder has resumed the apelike, knuckle-dragging posture (see the evolutionary chart below). In fact, to propel itself across short, flat sections of snow, the Snowboarder will use its arms as front legs precisely the way a chimpanzee or gorilla will.

Luckily the Snowboarder has evolved its brain matter since ape times. This is evident in the way it has solved the problem of tearing clothing when dragging its knees, knuckles, and butt in the snow. No, it has not stopped doing those things. It's just made special trousers with pads in the knees and butt, as well as fashioned gloves that are meant to be dragged.

But it's not just posture that's changed in the North American Snowboarder. Certain physical traits have manifested themselves.

Consider the case of Sid Mercury. Sid was born ten years ago to a very young couple from Stratton, Vermont. Sid's parents, Slade and Shayla, were two of snowboarding's pioneers and as such were honored with a huge party when they fostered a child.

During a full-moon party and much Dionysian rejoicing, Shayla brought young Sid out of his swaddling and stood him on his first snowboard.

The crowd let out a gasp.

For it was evident that one of Sid's legs was nearly twice the size of the other. His right leg looked like a sapling, his left the base of an oak tree. It was his dad, Slade, who immediately saw the beauty of the situation. He promptly picked Sid up and turned him the other way on his board.

"He's a goofy footer, I guess," said Slade. "Kid's a born rider."

And so he was. By the age of three, Sid was ripping the pipe. At five he won a boardercross. As his fame increased, scientists and evolutionary specialists began to hear tell of the amazing Snowboarder who was born with one leg twice the size of the other.

After exhaustive studies, scientists concluded that, from riding on catwalks, traverses, and

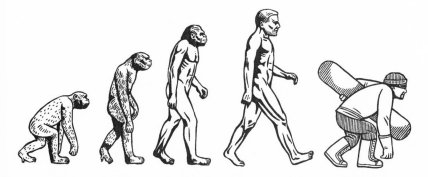

other flat stretches where the weight is held mostly on the back foot, longtime Snowboarders develop one huge leg. Snowboarders call this "riding the stump." Scientists call it Snowboardian Darwinism. Young Sid, who's become a Pro Bro, calls it a gift from God.

CHAPTER 18

The Snowboarder's Habitat

Three million years ago the prehistoric southern Africa hominid *Australopithecus africanus*—a squat, powerful, apelike being with long arms, strong, short legs, and a pitifully small brain—decided it didn't like being offered on the buffet of the veld.* Thus it began to build its homes in the trees. Dwelling in elaborate tree forts not unlike the one made popular thousands of years later in *Swiss Family Robinson,*† *Australopith-*

---

* A large, flat plain on which many species, including predators, live in constant conflict. A lot like many East Coast mountain resorts.

† A wonderful old movie in which a family of shipwrecked castaways live in a tree on a deserted island. Kind of like *Gilligan's Island* without the sumptuous Ginger.

ecus africanus was able to see predators coming from a long way off. It defended against these predators by throwing buckets of offal* down upon any being that tried to ascend to its lair.

This species might have lived amongst the branches indefinitely if it had not grown bored with eating its surroundings: leaves, bark, and other *Australopithecus africani.* In one of the earliest cases of how-are-you-going-to-keep-them-down-on-the-farm-once-they've-seen-the-bright-lights-of-the-city, some *Australopithecus africanus* came down out of the trees to get a brontosaurus burger.† It didn't take long after the first few tree dwellers tasted a medium rare burger; soon all the *Australopithecus africani* had descended.

---

* Picture a bunch of prehistoric Snowboarders living in a tree with neither outhouse nor national health standards. Now picture what would accumulate in those buckets (pronounced the same as "awful").

† This fact has led anthropologists to believe Fred Flintstone was actually an *Australopithecus africanus.*

Once back on the ground the *Australopithecus africanus,* with its small brain and short legs, was easy prey for hundreds of fleet-footed predators. Tragically the *Australopithecus africanus* was soon obliterated from the face of the earth. And all because it wanted a good burger.

The modern-day *Singleplankus ripthehillicus,* driven by law enforcement, mandated public codes of hygiene, and societal pressures for it to find a job, has likewise fled the flat plains and found refuge in snow-covered mountains.

There it lives in small, dark caves,* festooned with largely out-of-focus posters of other Snowboarders. It stacks the corners of its caves with as many slippery-bottomed boards as it can find. This not only takes up carpet space, meaning Snowboarders don't have to vacuum there, but the boards prevent rodents from climbing up the corners in their quest to get off the filthy carpet.

The couch is the focal point of any Snowboarder den. For this is not only where the Snowboarder spends its nonriding time but where it entertains, mates, and feeds. The longer a Snowboarder stays in one place, the more its couch is

* Also known as condominiums.

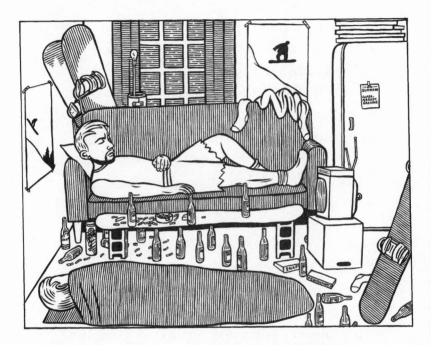

sprayed with various viscous substances (taco sauce, snowboard wax, excrement). The Snowboarder's couch gradually becomes quite slippery. So slick, in fact, that the Snowboarder may have a hard time staying on it.

This is not a bad thing. In fact, the Snowboarder likes this condition. It has given rise to a whole new sport: couch surfing. In this sport the Snowboarder attempts to stay on the couch's slick slouching space without ever taking its eyes off the television set or losing its grip on its Mountain Dew or Pringle's.

The advent of couch surfing has caused the Snowboarder to dwell for incredibly long periods (the whole summer) indoors. With the exception of daily winter excursions to ride the mountains, the Snowboarder never leaves its lair. Although small-brained like the *Australopithecus africanus*, the Snowboarder has learned from its ancestor's mistake; it never goes out to feed.

In fact the only way that vengeful skiers and DEA agents have been able to penetrate the lair of the Snowboarder is by dressing up in the distinctive red, white, and blue of the Domino's pizza deliveryman. This is also why many a Domino's deliveryman looks like he's been defiled with buckets of offal.

CHAPTER 19

Migratory Patterns

Weber will never sell gas grills to Snowboarders. Electric garage door opener companies and Toro riding-lawn-mower salesmen might as well delete Snowboarders from their databases. No, the North American Snowboarder is just not a nesting species. A Snowboarder setting up shop in the suburbs is about as likely as a militiaman going to work for the Internal Revenue Service.

The North American Snowboarder is a nomad, a vagabond. The Snowboarder chases snowstorms from resort to resort, and has been known to decamp instantly at the mention of free food—even if that food is a thousand miles away.

Yes, the migratory patterns of the North American Snowboarder are nothing if not predictable. As the first snows fly, the North American Snowboarders will awaken. Some have assumed cover identities for the summer, others have traveled to the Southern Hemisphere, but the true Snowboarder has slept on its couch from July until late October.

Once awakened from TV delirium and *Brady Bunch* rerun hibernation by the sound of snowplows, the Snowboarder will grab three things: its board, a bag containing all its worldly posses-

sions (snowboard boots, snowboard tool, a copy of this book), and its mandatory Snowboarder beanie (see Chapter 12). Next the Snowboarder will journey toward snow.

Its initial destination could be any of a hundred spots—from Big Bear or Brighton to Bolton; from Waterville Valley to Winter Park; from Hunter to Squaw—anywhere there is white, slippery, sloping land.

Yet when December rolls around every Snowboarder in the Northern Hemisphere will travel to Vail or Aspen. For it is here that the Snowboard industry holds its annual conference.

This is not just a trip for the Snowboarder, it is a pilgrimage. For this is where the tycoons of the snowboard industry gather to discuss important things like "What color are this year's beanies?" This, like Mecca, is where true believers come to bow down before their god. The Snowboarder's god? Sponsorship.

The North American Snowboarder will often travel in excess of 3,000 miles just to bow down and utter one sentence: "Dude, can ya hook me?"

The next time Snowboarders flock together is in the icy grayness of Stratton Mountain in February. The U.S. Open of Snowboarding is the excuse. Halfpipe and racing competitions take place. Everyone who's anyone in snowboarding is there, ostensibly to participate or watch. And of course the true reason the Snowboarder comes is to see who got hooked with what in December.

From the bone-chilling cold of Vermont, the Snowboarder begins a trek that takes it through the mountains of Colorado and Utah and countless 7-Eleven burrito dinners, until it winds up in the shimmering heat of Las Vegas in March.

There, in Sin City (appropriately enough), is where the snowboard industry meets to sell its wares and visit strip clubs in search of spokesmodels.

In a building big enough to house a battleship, manufacturers meet with retailers and wage a pitched battle with thousands of North American Snowboarders who've journeyed to the desert to bow down and utter one sentence: "Dude, can ya hook me?"

The final ceremonial meeting ground for the North American Snowboarder is in Colorado on the Continental Divide. In the mud parking lot of Arapaho Basin, thousands of North American Snowboarders gather. There, with speakers on the roofs of cars, with cheap keg beer flowing like biblical quotes at a Methodists' Sunday meeting, the Snowboarder communes with its fellow riders.

From the Cinco de Mayo celebration, where Snowboarders swing at skiers like they were piñatas, until the Fourth of July, A-Basin is the place for the Snowboarder to camp in the parking lot and ride the continent's dividing range in a great celebration of unity. This is a time when brothership flourishes amongst Snowboarders and plans are laid for the following season.

And it is a place to which Snowboarders journey thousands of miles to utter one sentence: "Dude, who will hook me next year?"

CHAPTER 20

Favored Transportation of the Snowboarder

When most people think of Snowboarder transportation they think of rusted-out microbuses or Subarus that saw their introduction around the time John Travolta was dancing on neon floors. In other words, most people think Snowboarders drive old, decrepit sh--boxes.

What a horrible generalization! This completely ignores many valid forms of Snowboarder transport—namely, the skateboard, the police car, and the thumb.

But before we get to those, let's talk about why Snowboarders drive sh--boxes. It's not because they are cheap or cooler or have more character, it's because they break down all the time. Now, most people would find this a real hindrance, but not Snowboarders. This is their cue that it's time to go clothes shopping.

Clothes shopping? How could driving around in a sh--box that breaks down all the time and clothes shopping possibly be connected?

Simple. The broken-down hulk is towed, with the Snowboarder, into a service station. In the service station are men wearing styley retro uniforms with names stitched into the pockets. The Snowboarder desires to look like these guys (for reasons discussed in Chapter 14).

This the Snowboarder can easily accomplish by slipping into the locker room in the back of the shop and filching the togs of some unsuspecting grease monkey.

Since Snowboarder cars often lose mufflers on bumpy mountain roads, it's no mystery why so many Snowboarders are seen riding the slopes in Midas muffler overalls.

Often as not the Snowboarder makes the grab while the guys are still working on its car. This brings up the second form of Snowboarder transport: the skateboard. With a few shoves the Snowboarder is rolling out of Midas and on its way to the mall to show off its new togs.

This, as if you didn't see it coming, brings up

the third most popular form of Snowboarder transport: the police cruiser. Directives have been issued in slope-side station houses all over the country to watch out for Snowboarders wearing Midas muffler uniforms while riding skateboards.

After it's been jailed, and the boys at Midas have sledgehammered its car, the Snowboarder takes to using its thumb for transport. It's at this stage that it's usually picked up by another Snowboarder in a junker on the way to shop for clothes at Midas.

THE ULTIMATE SNOWBOARDER VEHICLE

The Ultimate Snowboarder Vehicle is an old school bus. This gives the Snowboarder not only the room to carry all its riding bros but *huge* space to affix its stickers to. This way the bus can become a billboard as well as the Snowboarder's home.

Beds can be bolted to the floor,* a refrigerator installed, and most important, many couches can be moved in. Showers and toilets, of course, are optional equipment.

* An advantage not only on sharp corners but during frenzied Snowboarder sex.

BOOK IV

How to Become
a Snowboarder

CHAPTER 21

Adopting the Right Attitude

Attitude not only defines the North American Snowboarder but shapes its every response, colors its every mood. As such, it is the most important single ingredient in the twisted recipe for cooking oneself into a true Snowboarder.

You often hear of "bad attitude." This term is generally applied to petulant high schoolers or terminal adolescents and has nothing to do with the North American Snowboarder.

Really.

Then there is "good attitude," which is often used to describe merit-badge-winning Girl Scouts or successful encyclopedia salesmen. This description, quite obviously, also has nothing to do with the North American Snowboarder.

No, neither of these catchall terms comes close to describing the Snowboarder's bent or general demeanor. In fact, the Snowboarder doesn't have any attitude per se.

Not even, dude.

Rather, the North American Snowboarder has a 'tude. That's right, a 'tude. This is much more aggressive than any  mere schoolboyish "atti- tude." A 'tude is severed attitude. It's edgier, sharper. A 'tude is the sawed- off shotgun, the brass knuckles of the demeanor world. And it is something that every Snow- boarder is packing.

Beware the Snowboarder. It's got a 'tude in its baggies.

"Copping a 'tude" is the mental indoctrination to the Snowboarder's cult. It is to the Snow- boarder what baptism is to the Christian. It is a dunk in the waters of "whateverness."

Not sure what that means?

Let me see if I can't clear the sullied waters. "Whatever" is the Snowboarder's catchall, and it is the most obvious sign that a Snowboarder has properly copped a 'tude. With this one word the Snowboarder can answer any question.

"What do you want to do today, Bobby?"

"Whatever."

The Snowboarder can use this weapon to halt any discussion.

"Didn't you know that trail was closed?"

"Whatever."

Or disarm any dangerous query.

"Don't you love me, Jake?"

"Whatever."

See how copping a 'tude makes life so much simpler? One word, one notion, for all situations.* The 'tude blows past the trivialities of life (work, relationships, ski patrollers) and allows the North American Snowboarder to get on with what really matters: riding a snowboard.

Once a neophyte has copped a 'tude, there is no bringing it back. This is principally because non-Snowboarder communication is no longer possible. And, of course, Snowboarder communication is actually noncommunication (more on this in the next chapter).

---

* Which may make the Snowboarder well suited for American politics.

So, a Snowboarder with a proper 'tude is a Snowboarder for life. You'd sooner tattoo the pope with a 666 across his forehead than strip a Snowboarder of its essential 'tude.

Still don't get it?

Whatever, dude.

CHAPTER 22

How to Talk
the Talk

Would a dog be a dog if it couldn't bark? Could a mockingbird be a mockingbird if it could not sing? Perhaps. But never could these mute mutants be members of their species in the truest sense.

The same is true of the North American Snowboarder.

In order to be truly one of the species, it must be able to converse in Snowboarder-ese.* This is where many an aspiring Snowboarder falls flat. The reason wanna-be Snowboarders never pick

---

* Also known as boardhead, plankpatter, and jibberjive.

up the patois, never get into the cult, is because they are confused as to what Snowboarder Speak actually is.

They think it is communication. This is where they are dead wrong. The North American Snowboarder is not trying to communicate any-thing (other than the fact that he/she is a North American Snowboarder) with its speech. It is making noises, to be sure, but the sounds are not meant to convey meaning.

Consider the following sentence, which I over-heard at the base of the pipe: "Dude, way not phat. Vert's kinked, hit's boag-ed, and that wank just boned where I was ollie-ing."

Now most aspiring Snowboarders would try to decipher what was said, then reply with a co-gent remark. A response to this nonstatement, however, would shock the first dude. He was just spewing a collection of sounds. Any sensible re-sponse instantly brands the respondee as a wanna-be. It is then that the Snowboarder will throw his lit Camel no-filter in your face.

So, what to do?

Easy, don't listen. When a Snowboarder begins speaking to you, start constructing sentences of Snowboarder terms (see Glossary) in your head.

It doesn't actually matter what a Snowboarder says to you. Replying with something like "Dude, boyz be bustin pipe, boned for megaphats" will do fine.

The wonderful thing about Snowboarder-ese, like Swahili, is the words can be placed in any order at all. Thus the preceding sentence can just as effectively be uttered: "Boyz be boned bustin dude with megaphat pipe."

Of course, one must be careful to use such sentences only in conversation with a Snowboarder (who won't think to look for meaning).

When you're sure the meaning of your words amounts to absolutely nothing, when your speech inspires glassy-eyed nods from other Snowboarders and cheek-reddening frustration from non-Snowboarders, you know you've got it.

Why do they call snowboarding "snowboarding"? "Waste of time" was already taken.

CHAPTER 23

How to Walk
the Walk

Snowboarders don't walk. They don't stroll or amble. Snowboarders bounce and roll on their feet. They move like a well-oiled Snoop Doggy Dogg.* Now many think this is an affected means of locomotion derived from too many hours of watching *Yo! MTV Raps.*†

Truth is, the Snowboarder bounce/roll strut got its start in mud parking lots on both coasts. You see, the first areas to admit Snowboarders didn't have pavement. If you were an early riser,

---

* A lanky rap star with a caninelike gait to match his name.
† A television show in which cars bounce up and down and Snowboarder clothes are worn.

you could count on a getting a spot close to the lift, maybe even hitting the lot while the mud was still frozen. But because snowboarding's pioneers were wont to party into the morning hours, they didn't generally get to the areas early enough to catch the frozen muck.

Their cars squished and slopped in knee-deep glop until they could find a spot, sometimes half a mile from the lift. Whereupon the Snowboarders would bounce/hop to the lift. This became the generally accepted snowboard walk. It has been refined through continuous imitation to a springy pimp roll, but it will still get you through the mud with a minimum of splatter on your new baggies.

CHAPTER 24

How to Carry a Snowboard

The way a Snowboarder carries a board is telling. When hiking up the hill, virtually every type of rider (except the Carver) totes its stick across the small of its back. Carrying the board this way requires both hands to hook behind the back and the upper trunk to bend over. This causes Snowboarders to take on the posture and manner of slaves pulling a yoke. Which suggests that most riders are slaves to their boards. They are not the masters of their destiny, merely the objects of their boards' whims. The metaphor is apt.

This is not a stretch, really.

Consider skiers. They lug their sticks over their shoulders like rifles. Carvers hang their boards by leashes off their shoulders like arrow quivers.

The inference is that skiers and Carvers arm themselves to do battle with the mountain, to force it to succumb to their will. Freeriders come unarmed and ready to surf anything the mountain throws at them. So the Snowboarder is actually part of a quite benevolent tribe, unless, of course, it is packing a piece (which you'd never detect under the baggy clothes). That is a whole 'nother story.

CHAPTER 25

The Cool Daddy Handshake

Like the Masons or Elks, Snowboarders have a secret handshake that must be performed to gain entry into the club. It's known as the Cool Daddy Handshake. At the risk of death, possible excommunication from the Snowboarder fold, and the repo* of my handy Snowboarder tool, I'll reveal it.

Composed of three separate moves, the Cool Daddy Handshake will tell other Snowboarders that you are an initiate.

---

* Short for repossession. Also a quasi-hip reference to the cult classic *Repo Man,* which happens to be on the Snowboarder's must-see movie list.

It goes like this:

With your thumb up, reach out and grasp the other Snowboarder's hand. This is the same as what used to be known as a soul handshake. After you have grasped the other's hand, shake it once. That's one beat. Not down and up, just one down beat.

Next loosen your grip and slide your hand back so that your fingers meet its fingers. Now curl your fingers back toward you and hook its fingers (which will be curled away from you).

Perform one down beat with your fingers curled together.

Now comes the tricky part.

Unhook your fingers and begin to slide them back, away from the other's. The trick here is to put pressure on your fingers as you rapidly slide them away. As soon as they slip free, allow your top two fingers to whack against your thumb. This will make a snapping sound.

This sound, like that of your snowboard bonking off a ski patroller's head, proves you're cool.

CHAPTER 26

How to Choose Sunglasses

Since image is everything to the North American Snowboarder, choosing the appropriate pair of sunglasses is of utmost importance. These must not only protect the Snowboarder's eyes from the sun but also make the proper statement.*

An aspiring Snowboarder does not want to look like a state patrol officer (in Ray-Ban aviators) or an Indy pit crew boss (Gargoyles plastic shields).

The shades should roughly match the contour of the face (round for round faces, square for square faces). Lenses should be interchangeable,

---

* "I am a Snowboarder, touch me and prepare to die."

or the Snowboarder should own more than one pair of shades. As these are not to be taken off, you'll want the best possible lens for every type of light (including late-night bar light).

After many Snowboarders were shocked to see the people with whom they'd gone home from a late-night party, yellow and clear lenses became increasingly popular.

What follows is a list of sunglasses that are desirable to today's optically discerning and fashion-conscious Snowboarders.

SNOWBOARDER SUNGLASSES
- Oakley Eye Jacket or Trenchcoat
- Bollé Madness or Snake
- Arnet
- Black Flys
- Smith
- Briko (these racy shades are best for the Carver)
- Nikon Tetons
- Bugz Lunaz

CHAPTER 27

How to Move
to the Mountains

So you're ready to make the ultimate commitment: moving to the mountains.

You're ready to kiss all your "Real World" distractions good-bye and follow your soul. Congratulations, you've just taken the final step to becoming a lifelong Snowboarder.

Although it's a well-worn path, the journey won't be easy. First you must break the news to the parents, spouse, children, and friends you're about to lose.

Your father will most likely say: "I just paid $60,000 for your college tuition so you can become a *snowboarder*!"

Your mother will say: "Oh, honey, please. Mr. Manowankiwitz has a nice job waiting for you down at the bank."

Your spouse will say: Nothing. Expect a call from a divorce lawyer.

Your children will say: "Right on, Dad!" Until you inform them that they're going to boarding school* in Connecticut. At which point they will say: Nothing. Expect a call from *their* lawyers.

The correct Snowboarder response to all of these situations is a laconic "Whatever, dude."

Once you've shorn all those needless tethers that bound you to the "Real World,"† you're ready to journey to the mountains. The best time to go is September. This is a major changeover month in the mountains. Young people who have crumbled under the pressure from parents and friends are just departing to reenlist in "Real World" activities.

This may free up housing, but don't count on it.

Once you get to town, the first thing you'll

---

* Not snowboarding school.

† I put this in quotation marks to indicate it is an oft-used term. It is used to signify a place where people live but don't want to, spend their days toiling at jobs they wouldn't choose, and look forward to the ABC *Movie of the Week*.

need is shelter. You might try going to the local real estate agents. That is, until you see the small signs taped to their front doors that read:

SNOWBOARDERS NEED NOT APPLY

Next, check the classified ads in the local newspaper. Here you will find many skis for sale,* several dozen homes for sale,† but no rental properties. The local espresso bar is the next stop. Here you will find a few flyers tacked to the bulletin board announcing ROOMS FOR RENT or ROOMMATE NEEDED. Along the bottom of these flyers will be many tiny copies of a phone number, separated by small slits. You are meant to rip off a tab, take it with you to the phone, and dial up the number.

Under no circumstances should you do this. The reason? Anyone with the patience, organizational skills, and dexterity to set up this elaborate number-tab system is obviously not a Snowboarder.

---

* Mostly by skiers who've seen the light and switched to snowboarding.
† You'll quickly figure out that for the expense of a one-bedroom condo you could buy a small palace in the town you just moved from.

Next, call Domino's and ask if they've delivered any pizzas to a small, noisy village of tents. Follow the deliveryman's directions to the Snowboarders' encampment and pitch your tent. You will be with kindred spirits here. Answer any query with "Right on" and you're in. This Snowboarder commune will be a pleasant place to stay for a while.

Once you've secured a place to hang your beanie, get a job. The employer will know you're a Snowboarder, so you will be given a low-end position.* The good news is, you won't begin working for six weeks, until just before Thanksgiving. This gives you plenty of time to hang with your Snowboarder comrades and live in abject poverty.

During this period it is advisable to visit as many bars as possible. While alcohol consumption may facilitate sleeping in your tent, these frequent saloon visits will also accomplish another goal: finding a permanent home.

You will begin to notice large pods of Snowboarders moving together from bar to bar. Some

---

* The same kind of job that is called "entry level" in the "Real World."

will have pine needles and pitch stains on their baggies. Disregard these creatures. They are living in tents just like you.

Instead, find the ones whose clothes smell like cigarettes. These are the Snowboarders with homes. Stalk this group. Make friends with them. Then, once you've established yourself in their midst, discreetly follow them home. During the late-night housewarming ceremony,* slip in and find an empty corner. Put your sleeping bag down here. Erect a wall of bottles around your new encampment and lie down. Odds are no one will notice you until spring.

Now you have a home and a job. You are beyond the reach of parents and dependents, the IRS, and any creditors you might have accrued back in the "Real World." Congratulations, you have successfully moved to the mountains. You are now a true Snowboarder.

REASONS TO MOVE TO THE MOUNTAINS
• Proximity to snowboarding
• The chance to work in the guest services industry[†]

---

* The after-hours party.
[†] Also known as "tourist hell."

- Guaranteed poverty-induced weight loss program
- Two words: Board Bettys

THINGS TO LEAVE IN THE "REAL WORLD"
- Any clothes that aren't flannel or waterproof
- All pens, paper, and calculators*
- All non-Snowboarder friends, relatives, dependents
- Your TV remote control[†]
- Morals

WHAT TO BRING TO THE MOUNTAINS
- Snowboard gear
- Sense of humor
- Tent
- Sleeping bag
- Enough nonperishable food to last the winter
- Medical supplies (to splint broken thumbs)

---

* You won't need a calculator to keep track of your earnings, believe me.
[†] This will be very difficult for most aspiring Snowboarders, but it won't do you much good in your tent anyway.

- Trust fund access code
- Girlfriend/boyfriend with a trust fund
- This book
- Truckload of empty beer and liquor bottles*

* To decorate your new home.

BOOK V

Tips for the
Non-Snowboarder

CHAPTER 28

How to Have a Relationship with a Snowboarder

This is an easy one. Don't.

Oh, it's too late. You're already trying to have a relationship with a Snowboarder. You're in *love* with a Snowboarder? Now we've got work to do.

First of all, examine your motives. Do you feel a pent-up need to punish yourself? Do you have a martyr complex? Are you afraid of successful relationships?

If you answered yes to any one of these questions, stop beating yourself up, put down this book, and call the Snowboard Lovers Anonymous Ministry (SLAM). If you were able to answer no to all those questions, you just might be a reasonably well-adjusted person who has inadvertently fallen in love with a Snowboarder.

What to do?

First, become a Snowboarder yourself. I know this sounds drastic, but it makes complete sense. Perhaps not for the reason you think, however. I'm not recommending this so you'll ever be able to ride with your Snowboarder. Heck no, he'll never let his bros see him riding with you. You may be able to coax him into a trip to Hunter Mountain, where he knows none of his friends would ever be caught dead, but you'll never persuade him to go up on his home hill with his girlfriend.

No, the reason to start 'boarding is not so you can share time on the hill, it's so you can elicit serious sympathy when your beloved sees the multiple abrasions you'll incur during the Snowboard Initiation Ceremony (also known as your first snowboard lesson, see Chapter 5).

This will work. Trust me. He will be all pathos, passion, and proffered Band-Aids for at least a day. Enjoy that day; it may be the best you'll ever get.

WHAT TO EXPECT FROM YOUR
SNOWBOARDER

1. When it snows, your Snowboarder disappears.

Your lover of last night disappears in a contrail of white spray, leaving you standing alone atop an expert run. Since you're smooching your Snowboarder, you assume the no-friends-on-a-powder-day rule* doesn't apply to you.

Well, the no-friends-on-a-powder-day rule was actually amended to fit the politically correct 1990s. It used to read, No girlfriends/boyfriends on a powder day. That *does* mean you.

Then you notice it's not just powder days that cause your Snowboarder to disappear. Every day there is snow on the ground the Snowboarder will somehow manage to pull a Houdini.

This becomes a problem only when you've made plans to do anything but snowboard. Here, the mistake is yours. The only sensible tactic when planning for shared time with a Snow-

---

* The irrefutable rule that states a Snowboarder never waits for anyone—best friend, business partner, grandmother—when there is new snow to be ridden. This may be the first time it's been put in print.

boarder is to slate events from July until late October. These are the only months in which the
North American Snowboarder will not be riding
the snow-covered mountains.

The difficulty in planning during these months
is that the Snowboarder will more than likely
sleep through its hibernation period.

Or worse: The Snowboarder will be awake but
seem to be Super-Glued to the couch.

2. Your Snowboarder will not get off the couch.

Here you have two options: surf the couch together or resort to serious trickery.

A tried-and-true method is "the Potato Flake
Fake." Get several boxes of dehydrated potato
flakes and create an outdoor perch above the
window nearest the couch. Next, have a friend
tie a metal object (a mailbox works fine, particularly a big blue postal service one) to the car and
drag it down the road. This sound will activate
something deep inside the cortex of your couch-
bound Snowboarder, who will think it's a snowplow. When he looks out the window, begin
dumping the potato flakes.

When he goes for the shed where the snowboard is, jump your Snowboarder and cover his

face with a rag soaked in chloroform. He will promptly pass out. Now you've got him. Sure, he's unconscious, but this will have to pass for quality time. You know as soon as he wakes up, he'll head for that couch.

3. Your Snowboarder can only make love in a gondola.

This is a very common Snowboarder malady (see Chapter 11). You have two choices. Buy a season pass and throw away your reputation (if you have any left after having announced to your friends that you are in love with a Snowboarder). Or, with a simple welding torch and a truckload of sheet metal, rebuild your bed to resemble a gondola.

When doing so, however, take care to reproduce it in the most minute detail. Be sure to affix a sticker that originally read, "Thank you for not smoking," but now (thanks to a Snowboarder with a pen) reads, "Thank you for pot smoking," on your headboard.

If that doesn't work, hire someone to check tickets just outside your bed-gondola. If even that doesn't work, get drastic by having fully attired skiers pile into the bed-gondola with you.

4. His Tongue Stud Gives Him Stainless Steel Breath

You give your Snowboarder a big smooch and his lips taste like a chrome bumper. The problem of stainless steel breath stems not from the stud but from the nasty polish that your Snowboarder uses to clean it.

Take heart, this problem has recently been solved by the legendary Mr. Zog,* who's recently come out with a line of tongue-stud steel polish. I recommend the wonderful new flavor: masochistic mint. Buy your man a can. He'll love ya for it.

5. Your Snowboarder Brings His Board to Bed

Not many women want three in their bed, but that's just the situation you're confronted with, because no real Snowboarder can leave his first love, his snowboard, in a cold locker or drafty garage.

This brings up the question: Who or what is the most important thing in the Snowboarder's life? This is so obvious, so elemental, that the question need not even be asked. The Snow-

---

* Mr. Zog also manufactures Sex Wax, which actually has nothing to do with copulation but has become very popular with surfers who don't know that.

boarder will always give the nod to the one who does not ask the question. Since his snowboard is inanimate, you, dear heartthrob, will surely be the loser in this contest.

Well, let's say you can live with that. You'll play second fiddle to a Hooger Booger.*

So he brings the board to bed, big deal.

Beware, however, because there's more at stake than mere green-eyed jealousy. There's a real safety problem here. Snowboard edges can be very sharp; you may well end up cuddling up to something resembling a Wilkinson Sword blade. If you don't get sliced to ribbons, your sheets surely will.

My advice is to buy a padded snowboard bag and bring it to bed with you. Tell your Snow-boarder that it's so you can "tuck baby board in." Now it won't bother you until morning. With the baby in the snowboard bag, the gon-dola door latched shut, and the ticket checkers on break, you can make wonderful Snowboarder love. Until, of course, the snowplow goes by.

* A brand of snowboard. Really.

CHAPTER 29

How to Rent a House to a Snowboarder

Say you're a non-Snowboarder who either has a spare bedroom or owns a rental condo. A Snowboarder answers your ad.

Sure, his nose ring throws you a bit, and the bitchin' shades that he always wears give you pause, but he seems okay enough. And, heck, you're open-minded.

So you get the first and last month's rent money up front and offer to help him move in. Fortunately, as he has only his snowboard and a boot bag, he doesn't need your help.

For the first few weeks he's as quiet as a church mouse. In fact, it doesn't seem as though he's left the place. He pays the rent on time. You're happy.

Then it snows.

Suddenly the one goateed guy you rented to seems to have cloned himself. There are seven of him now. They're all staying in your previously pristine condo.

You look in the window. Where there once was a kitchen counter, a beer bottle forest has sprung up. A crop of cigarette butts has been planted in the carpet. The couch is covered with what appear to be dead bodies. A snowboard vise is screwed onto the dining room table.

A sculpture resembling the Leaning Tower of Pisa, and made exclusively of Domino's pizza boxes, has been erected in the corner. Seven Midas muffler jackets are draped over what used to be the kitchen stove. As the season wears on, the cloning continues. Soon a whole flock of Snowboarders are roosting in your unit.

The police visit regularly. The Board of Health is leaving nasty messages on your machine. The neighbors have burned you in effigy.

You consider suicide.

Then, one day, it mercifully stops snowing.

The clones—of which there are now thirty-seven—vanish. You have the last month's rent, but you have to bulldoze the place and completely rebuild.

How could this have happened to me? you wonder.

A better question would be: How can you prevent this from ever happening again?

The first thing you do differently is take snowboards for a security deposit.* This assures you that the Snowboarder will not skip out (or at least that you'll have something to ride in your newfound poverty).

Next, rent the place with the beer bottle forest, the Leaning Tower of Pisa, and the cigarette crop already in place. These are necessary decor for any Snowboarder. There's no getting around them, and they're not altogether aesthetically unappealing.

The problem with these icons of the Snowboarder domain is the damage caused to your place during their creation ceremonies.† Therefore, if you stock your condo with all the accoutrements of the Snowboarder's habitat before he

---

* Be sure they are up to date. A rope attached at the nose or metal tail fins are bad signs.
† Also known as after-hours parties.

gets in there, he won't have to hold these ceremonies.

And, take heart, when the last chairlifts stop
running, your Snowboarder problems will also
melt away like spring snow. Unless, of course, the
Snowboarder decides to hibernate in your rental
unit. At this point you have no recourse. Bulldoze
the sucker.

FIVE REASONS TO RENT TO A SNOWBOARDER
1. Good revenge on your neighbors
2. Devalues your home and lessens your tax burden
3. An extra $1,000 in nickel-deposit beer bottles
4. More police presence in the neighborhood
5. You'll get to see a bulldozer at work

CHAPTER 30

How to Raise a Snowboarder (Without It Ending Up in Jail)

So your offspring wants to become a Snow-boarder. A parent's nightmare. You fear the tat-toos and piercings will stigmatize your child, doom him/her to a life of endless dead-end resort jobs, baggy trousers, and stainless steel breath.

For this reason you refuse to buy your child a snowboard. You balk when he/she wants Tommy Hilfiger jeans six sizes too large. You force your child onto skis. This will keep the little nipper from ever single-planking, right?

Dead wrong.

To raise a child that isn't completely addicted to snowboarding, you must become a Snowboarder yourself. Truncate your twenty-two-year IBM career, move to the mountains, and morph into a *Singleplankus r. teachthechumpsicus,* otherwise known as a Snowboard Instructor. Dye your hair green, get a few tattoos, and start chaining your wallet (which will be suitably empty) to your hip.

At first your child will think you're way cool. Go with it. Buy the kid not only freestyle boards but a carving stick and a huge powder plank. Provide the kid with nonpermanent stick-on tattoos, clip-on nose rings, and magnetic cheek studs.

Make sure you wear the same tattoos and studs as your child does. Every day.

One day (at around age thirteen) your child will look up at you and be repulsed. Not because you're ugly, mind you. He will be repulsed at himself for turning out (at thirteen he'll think he's all grown up) like you.

At this point he will throw his baggies in the trash and plead with you to buy him some button-down oxfords, Brooks Brothers suits, and several pairs of wingtips.

And you, dear parent, have turned a Snowboarder into a Young Republican. Sure, you had to ruin your life to do it, but who's more important? You or the future of this country?

Oh yes, make no mistake about it, your child constitutes the future. He'd better, because you, with your green hair, tattoos, and empty wallet, have absolutely none. Take heart, however, for every day you masquerade as a Snowboard Instructor is another day you get to slam wanna-be Snowboarders on their faces.

CHAPTER 31

How to Employ a Snowboarder

I can just hear you: "Why would I ever want to employ a Snowboarder?"

Simple. In mountain towns, the labor force is thin. Because of astronomical rental rates, the ski bums of yesteryear* can no longer afford to live in resort towns. Snowboarders, on the other hand, have adapted to the exorbitant rents by piling impossible numbers of 'boarders into a single condominium, then splitting the rent between, say, thirty-seven people. Mountain-town rents are almost affordable when 'boarders do that.

So you're faced with hiring either a Snow-

---

* Those dudes with the stretch pants and white zinc on their lips.

boarder or no one at all. If closing your business isn't a viable option, go ahead and hire the Snowboarder.

But first a few caveats.

You'll want to avoid any conflict with the Snowboarder. Why? Because your job, no matter how good it may be, is only a means to keep the Snowboarder snowboarding. If your place becomes a place of hassle, the Snowboarder will decamp and go back to Taco Bell.

So, here are a few conflict avoidance techniques:

• Do not schedule the Snowboarder for any time when the lifts are open. It will skip out if you do.

• Provide bonuses in the form of snowboard mitts, wax, or the ever-popular multihead snowboard tool.

• In order to profit from the Snowboarder's unusual appearance, run contests to guess which color its hair will be next week.

• Offer free piercings with your health plan.

• Install a huge couch and a forest of empty beer bottles in the dimly lit back room. Allow the Snowboarder to spend breaks and summers in this room.

1. Thou shalt not miss a powder day.
2. Thou shalt not covet thy neighbor's board.
3. Thou shalt not wear a suit.
4. Thou shalt not take off thy beanie.
5. Thou shalt not remove thy shades.
6. Thou shalt never ski.
7. Thou shalt not hold a day job.
8. Thou shalt not remove a tattoo.
9. Thou shalt begin and end every sentence with "dude" or "right on."
10. Thou shalt not bathe during winter.

A

aggro (adjective) describes something done in a very enthusiastic manner. Short for "aggressive."

Airwalks (proper noun) a brand of snowboarding boots and sneakers.

Air Dog (noun) a Snowboarder who is primarily interested in catching air.

B

backside (noun) the edge of the snowboard where the heels rest.

(adjective) describes anything that contacts the

backside edge, e.g., backside air, backside wall, and so on.

baggies (noun) loose-fitting trousers worn by the Snowboarder.

bail (verb) to exit.

beat (adjective) describes something not good.

bindings (noun) devices that attach the Snow-boarder to its board.

boag (verb) to make bogus; to ruin.

Board Betty (noun) a female Snowboarder.

Board Bro (noun) a male Snowboarder.

boardercross (noun) a competition in which Snowboarders race through a snowboard park, four or six at a time, with no rules. Part roller derby, part downhill.

bone (verb) to accentuate. Same definition for "bone it out."

bonk (verb) to hit a hard object.

boost (verb) to catch air out of the halfpipe.

boyz (noun) a group of men with adolescent mind-sets and baggy clothing.

brah (noun) a male Snowboarder. Slang for "brother."

bust (verb) to initiate something. "Bustin a move" is beginning an exit.

C

carve (verb) to lacerate the hill with sharp turns on a snowboard.

cat out the window (noun) a jump in which the Snowboarder flails uncontrollably through the air.

Cool Daddy Handshake (noun) a greeting ritual performed by Snowboarders.

corduroy (noun) freshly groomed snow.

crater (verb) to land a jump very badly. "He totally cratered off that cliff."

D

duck-footed (adjective) describes a stance in which the toes point outward, like the feet of a duck.

dude (noun) person. Mandatory beginning and ending word in any Snowboarder sentence.

E

eggbeater (noun) a severe fall.
(verb) to tumble in a dramatic, often disastrous manner.

F

fakie (verb) to ride a snowboard backward.

fall line (noun) the straightest line down the hill.

flail (verb) to perform something very poorly.

flailer (noun) a person who regularly performs poorly.

flat bottom (noun) the base of the halfpipe or the rear end of a Snowboarder (from sitting on the ground too much).

Freerider (noun) a Snowboarder who does not compete but often does ride for money.

frontside (noun) the edge of the snowboard where the toes rest.

(adjective) describes anything that contacts the frontside edge, e.g., frontside air, frontside wall, and so on.

G

go off (verb) to do anything with extraordinary verve.

goofy footer (noun) a person who rides a snowboard with the right foot in the forward position.

grab (noun) a jump in which part of the snowboard is clutched by the hand.

grind (verb) to slide a snowboard down a rail, tree, or fallen skier in a direction perpendicular to the fall line.

grommet (noun) a young Snowboarder.

H

halfpipe (noun) a deep trough in the snow where Snowboarders perform freestyle maneuvers and courtship rituals.

heel-side (adjective) describes anything done employing the back edge of the snowboard, e.g., a heel-side turn.

hit (noun) a jump or spot where a trick can be performed.

hook (verb) to align someone with something. "That Burton dude just hooked me with a sweet sponsorship deal."

hospital air (noun) a jump so big that it threatens to make its pilot seek medical attention.

huck (verb) to jump recklessly.

huckfest (noun) a testosterone-fueled session in which riders try to catch bigger and bigger air.

I

Instructor (noun) a Snowboarder who feigns teaching the sport in order to screen out weak would-be riders.

invert (noun) a trick in which the Snowboarder goes upside down.

J

Jibber (noun) a freestyle rider.

K

kicker (noun) a jump.

kinked (adjective) describes an abrupt transition in the halfpipe.

L

lame (adjective) describes anything very uncool.

leash (noun) device attached to the front foot to keep the snowboard from sliding down the hill when the rider comes out of the bindings.

lip (noun) the top edge of a halfpipe or jump; talk that is abusive (what a Snowboarder will surely give you).

M

Mammoth Mountain (noun) a snowboarding mecca in California.

mega (adjective) describes something very big or good. See also "way."

N

new school (adjective) describes styles and techniques that are different from those of early Snowboarders.

noodle (noun) something soft. "That board was a total noodle."

nose poke (noun) a jump in which the airborne rider shoves the front tip of the nose forward.

O

old school (adjective) describes something that hearkens back to techniques and styles developed during snowboarding's formative years.

ollie (noun) a Snowboarder trick in which the tail of the board is slapped on the ground and used to spring into the air.

P

phat (adjective) describes something that is big or good in a soulful way.

pipe (noun) short for halfpipe. A sometime Snowboarder accessory.

(verb) to ride the halfpipe. "He was piping rad."

poach (verb) to steal an experience; riding a closed run is "poaching it."

poseur (noun) a person who pretends to be something he/she is not.

Pro Bro (noun) a Snowboarder who gets paid to snowboard and look disinterested in everything.

R

rail (noun) the edge of a snowboard.

(verb) to carve well, or to slide down an inanimate object, such as a tree, a pipe, or a lift operator.

S

skinny (noun) the truth.

ski patroller (noun) a red-clad skier with the authority to expel a Snowboarder from the lift-served hill.

Snowboarder (noun) a strange species of human that is characterized by riding a plank over snow and other aberrant behavior.

Snowboarder-ese (noun) the language spoken by Snowboarders. Incomprehensible, even to its speakers.

Snowboard spotter (noun) a person with no life who enjoys watching the North American Snowboarder in its native habitat.

spew (verb) to talk incessantly about oneself.

sponsor (noun) an entity that has too much money on its hands and thus pays Snowboarders to ride snowboards and wear patches.

T

tattoo (noun) skin design formed by injecting ink into the epidermal layer. Mandatory for any Snowboarder.

technician (noun) a highfalutin name for someone who performs a mundane task. A Hobart technician is a dishwasher; a snowboard technician is a hot-wax jockey.

thang (noun) slang for "thing." Denotes a soulful thing.

toe-side (adjective) describes something done using the front edge of the snowboard, e.g., a toe-side turn.

Tourist (noun) a person who spends inordinate amounts of money to visit a place where people disrespect him/her.

'tude (noun) the Snowboarder's attitude.

tweak (verb) to accentuate. "He really tweaked that back-side Indy."
Also to injure slightly. "I tweaked my ankle."
(adjective) off kilter. "That dude is totally tweaked."

V

vert (adjective) short for "vertical." Describes the upper edges of a halfpipe.

W

wank derogatory noun or masturbatory verb.

wanna-be (noun) a person who desires to become something else.

way (adjective) superlative meaning very, or a lot.

whatever (pronoun) when used as a Snowboarder's stock, vague answer to any question, it means, "I don't want to talk to you," or "I don't have a real answer."

X

xer (noun) a member of Generation X.

xtreme (adjective) the same as "extreme," just a real hip way to spell it.

Y

yahoo (noun) a person, often a Tourist, who behaves in a dangerous manner on the slopes.

Z

zoned (adjective) in a nonfocused state of mind. "That guy was so zoned that he didn't even know I took his snowboard."

Just as one might take a checklist on an African safari, the organized Snowboard spotter should bring this handy-dandy checklist into the field.

A sample entry has been made to give you the idea.

Subspecies	Place Spotted	Activity
√ Jibber	Vail Halfpipe	Courtship ritual
__ Jibber		
__ Carver		
__ EuroCarver		
__ Instructor		
__ Shop Rat		
__ Shop Rat Wanna-be		
__ Pro Bro		
__ Pro Betty		

AN EXHAUSTIVE LIST OF
SNOWBOARDER CONTRIBUTIONS
TO SOCIETY

BILL KERIG has been a contributing editor at both *Skiing* and *Snowboard Life* magazines. He is the host of the Weather Channel's *Private Lessons* ski and snowboard tips. He lives and rides in Vail, Colorado.